*Christians
in the Nicaraguan
Revolution*

Margaret Randall

Christians in the Nicaraguan Revolution

translated by Mariana Valverde

New Star Books
Vancouver

Canadian Cataloguing in Publication Data

Randall, Margaret, 1938-
    Christians in the Nicaraguan revolution

ISBN 0-919573-14-2 (bound). -- ISBN
    0-919573-15-0 (pbk.)

1. Catholic Church - Nicaragua - History.
2. Nicaragua - History - Revolution, 1979 -
Religious aspects. 3. Religion and politics -
Nicaragua. 4. Liberation theology. I. Title.
BX1442.2.R36 1983   282'.7285   C83-091356-4

The photo on page 97 is by Claudia Gordillo;
all other photographs are by Margaret Randall.

5   4   3   2   84   85   86   87

New Star Books Ltd.
2504 York Avenue
Vancouver, B.C.
Canada V6K 1E3

PRINTED AND BOUND IN CANADA

For my parents
John and Elinor
"love that grows like a poem"

Contents

Publisher's Note

The people at New Star Books wish to thank the many individuals and groups who contributed generously to the publication of *Christians in the Nicaraguan Revolution*. Among the contributors:

Marjorie Thibodeau, Rohan Samarajiwa, Lily Mah-Sen, Joyce Harris, Mary Ann Morris, David Behn, Rick Craig, Barbara Jenks, Barry Jenks, Phil Esmonde, Oxfam Canada, International Development Education Resources Association (IDERA), Ten Days for World Development (Victoria), Global Concerns, Sisters of Saint Ann (Victoria), Victoria Central America Support Committee, Cross Cultural Learner Centre, Latin American Working Group, Global Village (Nanaimo) and Ottawa Central America Solidarity Committee.

Acknowledgments

*M*any people helped to make this book. Kate Pravera worked on the rough draft of the sections on Solentiname and El Riguero. Her ability to extract the essentials and give the testimonies a coherent order is an important part of the finished work.

Preliminary discussions with Uriel Molina, Ernesto Cardenal, Teofilo Cabestrero, Luz Beatriz Arellano and Giulio Girardi were indispensable. Irene Barillas Montiel, Maritza Gonzalez, Lesbia del Socorro Rodriguez Bojorge and Pirjo Mikkonen helped to do the transcriptions and typing. And Jeanne Gallo, Diane Kenney, Robert Stark, Frei Betto and Michael Czerny were helpful in other ways.

For the English edition, Leslie Cotter, David Kidd, Liza McCoy, Frank Rooney, Jane Springer and my dear friend and editor Lynda Yanz put in endless hours without which the transition from a Latin American to North American audience would have been deficient indeed.

To all of these sisters and brothers, my love and commitment.

—M.R.

9

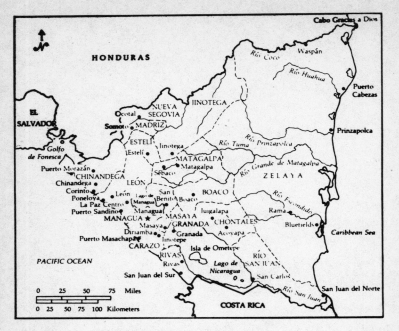

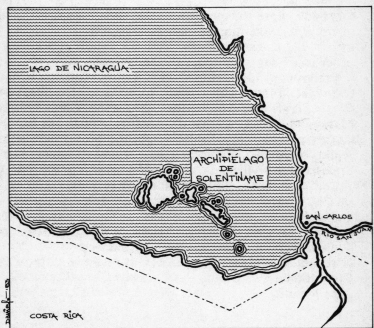

Introduction

You ask about my faith...
I answer with my life...
                    —*Pedro Casaldaliga*

*I*n Nicaragua, for the first time in modern history, the official church sided with an authentic popular revolution. Although there have been progressive Christians in other Latin American countries, Nicaragua is the first country where Christians as a group played a decisive role in all aspects of the political and social conflict up to and including armed struggle. Now in "peacetime," differences have emerged between the church's hierarchy and the Christian community at large, similar to political and class tensions in other sectors of Nicaraguan society.

This book tells the story of some of the exemplary men and women for whom the Christian vocation means complete revolutionary loyalty. It is also the story of two Christian base communities that played important roles in the revolutionary struggle. The first is the contemplative

11

community founded by Father Ernesto Cardenal in Our Lady of Solentiname, a remote group of islands in Lake Nicaragua. It functioned during the years 1966 to 1977, until the island community was destroyed by the National Guard after young people from the community took part in an FSLN action. The second, the so-called "university community" associated with Father Uriel Molina, was in the parish of Fatima in Managua's Riguero neighborhood. It began in 1971 on the initiative of a dozen university students, who felt the need to leave their middle-class homes and live among the people. Both experiences were key in the parallel efforts and growing unity of the FSLN and organized Christians in the Nicaraguan liberation struggle.

. . . religious feeling
is the function of a special organ of the
*   human body*
unknown until now, and one could
also say, therefore
that, at the exact moment when that
*   organ*
is fully functioning
the believer is so free from malice
as to seem almost like a plant
Oh soul! Oh thought! Oh Marx! Oh
*   Feuerbach!*
> *—Cesar Vallejo, from "At*
> *the moment when the tennis*
> *player. . ."*

Religious distress is at the same time the
expression of real distress and also the
protest against real distress. Religion is
the sigh of the oppressed creature, the

heart of a heartless world, just as it is the
spirit of spiritless conditions. It is the
opium of the people.
                                    —*Karl Marx*

So much has been said about that last sentence. And Marx's preceding sentences have been neglected, first of all by "armchair Marxists," but also by the church itself, which for centuries seems to have forgotten about its mission of protest.

I am a Marxist and an atheist. Yet in my contact with the Christian faith I have met some of the most committed revolutionaries that I have known in my life, a life in which it has been my privilege to know and learn from many revolutionaries. When I arrived in Nicaragua for the first time in October 1979, it was to do field work for a book about women in the revolution. That was my first contact with this country in upheaval, an experience which was deepened throughout my three month stay and then later when I returned to live here. In writing these lines, my experience is still beginning, after a little over a year. Among many other things my time here has served to draw me nearer to Christians in the revolution.

I come from a vaguely Jewish family. My upbringing contained elements of Christian Science, Quaker Sunday school classes, a brief encounter with a liberal Episcopalian parish and a good dose of pragmatism. I had minimal personal contact with Catholicism but certainly my initial grasp of it was that the Catholic Church — and Catholics themselves — lived according to norms quite different from those they preached. From my years in Spain I still remember stories about priests with hidden love affairs; from Mexico, I can recall images of rural hills crowned by majestic churches, emerging from and dominating the maddening misery of hopeless shacks.

The negativism associated with the Catholicism in my childhood, and then in Spain, Mexico and my twelve years in Cuba is in dramatic contrast to the love, security, the "rightness" or simply the "naturalness" which Catholicism involves for the immense majority of my friends in Nicaragua, those who speak in the pages of this book. I arrived in Nicaragua an amazed non-believing foreigner. In the time I have been here I think I have passed the supreme test involved in approaching and drawing closer to the world — although not, I confess, to the experience of Christian faith.

It still bothers me at times to be introduced in Christian circles as "our atheist". To be an atheist seems more of an omission than an affirmation. It points to the absence of a belief rather than to an affirmation of the dialectical materialism of my professed Marxism. I do believe, and deeply, in many extraordinary things: in life, in human beings, in the power of love — and of hatred. I believe in the irrevocable laws of history, and in the creativity of the men and women who apply them. However, I have not ever felt the need which in so many people translates itself into a belief in God, if by belief one understands the acknowledgement, the experience of a supreme being, an all-powerful and all-present power, or even the less intelligible experience of faith.

If I begin by talking about myself, my training and my ideas, it is because I think it is necessary to warn the reader about my prejudices, about the point of departure from which I look out on the powerful world of Christians in revolution. In that sense this introduction represents my own testimony about the subject as well as providing a context for the material that follows. I write about this topic from the only honest perspective which is possible for me: that of an outsider who approaches cautiously but who, in this drawing near, feels the awakening of a profound respect and even the beginnings of identification.

As I have struggled to understand the experience of Christians in Nicaragua many women and men of the church of the poor have provided guidance. They took me in with true Christian and revolutionary affection and gave me every kind of help, from simple information to the friendship that allows for deeper understanding. These same brothers and sisters warned me, on more than one occasion, about the dangers of my own idealism. It has been and continues to be a privilege to be able to live these times beside comrades who are committed to the revolutionary process and to their Christian faith. I am conscious of my responsibilities as a chronicler and as a sister.

It is absolutely essential for Marxist revolutionaries and Christian revolutionaries (as well as those who are both) to stop and examine what has happened, is happening and might yet happen in this long-suffering and victorious land, on this volcano that is healing itself and growing.

We speak of identical values. What are they?

Christianity sees human beings as brothers and sisters. The revolutionary struggle in Nicaragua has meant a significant use of the terms "brother" and "sister" among comrades, a practice that was also found in Sandino's time.

Both the Christian and the revolutionary see love as the basis for life. The Christian preaches the love of Jesus Christ. Commander Che Guevara, an example of future freedom in America, said, "At the risk of seeming ridiculous, let me say to you that the true revolutionary is guided by great feelings of love."

Christians cultivate humility. Humility and modesty are characteristics inherent in true revolutionaries. What could be a greater sacrifice than a life dedicated to struggle, or a mother's willingness to give up her child to the struggle?

Generosity is the supreme value for a Christian. The Sandinista Popular Revolution has been remarkable for its generosity.

The true Christian aspires to poverty as a way of showing solidarity with those who have less, and this is reflected in the norms of the majority of religious orders and congregations, whose members work collectively and share what is needed to survive. Revolutionary socialism creates the conditions for the sharing of material and spiritual goods equally among the population; under socialism individual good is subordinated to the general good.

Liberation theology, through its preferential option for the poor, recognizes that human beings need first of all to meet their basic needs for shelter, food and health, in order to meet other needs like education, culture and recreation. The socialist revolution, in winning workers control over the means of production as well as a just distribution of the product, ensures the satisfaction of both primary and secondary needs for the people.

Christians talk about the Resurrection, Christ's victory over death. They say that Jesus lives in us. The revolutionary affirms that heroes and martyrs have not died, but continue to live in a work that endures. And Marx, in the *Economic and Philosophical Manuscripts of 1844*, says, "Death seems to be the harsh victory of the species over the particular individual, and a contradiction in its unity. But the particular individual is only an individual of the species, and as such, is mortal."

Christians and revolutionaries fight to create the kingdom of God, which is increasingly interpreted to mean a better life for human beings. Christian revolutionaries, and revolutionaries who are not Christians, know that they can and ought to fight for a kingdom that begins with the work of human hands...and which may or may not continue on another level, open to discussion.

Through the testimonies that we read in this book, we see how these values are reflected in the daily lives of the revolutionaries in Nicaragua. A new relation between two visions is being born and a practice produced which has no precedents, at least not in modern history.

The church in Cuba

Christianity without apocalypsis, and
Marxism without transcendence, are two
heresies unnecessarily fighting against
each other.

—Carl Baaten

What about Cuba? It deserves separate treatment. The Cuban revolution developed and triumphed in the era before Vatican II, and furthermore, in a country in which the people did not have a profound Christian faith. Catholicism belonged to the wealthy strata of Cuban society. The people — poor, black, marginalized and dominated — expressed themselves more authentically through African rites such as *Yoruba* and the mysterious *Santaria*, norms which ruled vast groups economically, socially and spiritually.

The religion brought by the Africans who came as slaves to the Caribbean island was useful to them, often as the only allowable self-expression in the midst of a life that was extremely dark and full of anguish. Hence, the religion practiced by the Cuban masses, the faith that the bearded rebels carried with them to Sierra Maestra, was that of *Shango* as well as of St. Barbara, that of *Oggun* as well as the Madonna of Copper.

The institutional attitude of the Catholic church in Cuba, during the stuggle and at the triumph of the revolution, was faithful to its class interests. It wavered between an open hostility and a self-isolation. We only have a few cases of priests, religious and lay Christians who individually placed themselves on the side of social change. In this sense the relationship between church and state in Cuba must be understood within an analysis of the history of the world church, its classist manifestation in pre-revolutionary Cuba and the historical moment in which the triumph took place.

Although there is no religious persecution in revolutionary Cuba, and the socialist constitution (February, 1970) firmly condemns discrimination on the basis of religion, the Cuban Communist party does not accept believers as members. That is, a believer in Cuba can live, study, work and share all the rights and duties of any citizen, including the free expression and practice of her or his religious faith. But she or he cannot belong to the Cuban Communist Party because the party of the revolution demands a materialist conception of the world from its militants.

Yet Cuba did have an impact on the progressive church throughout Latin America. Cuba was the first socialist revolution in Latin America and continues to present an example for the Americas. Cuba's influence forced the church to re-evaluate its role in Latin America. It presented a clear alternative to religious piety as an answer for the poor and oppressed. Fidel Castro was one of the early political leaders to applaud the efforts of Christian activists and he often emphasized the common ground of socialists and revolutionary Christians. However, the Cuban church remained marginal, with respect not only to the revolution but also to the church in other Latin American countries, while in Nicaragua and elsewhere events were beginning to take place that would shape forever the nature of the church as a collective voice and expression of the faith of the peoples.

Liberation theology

The day that you people manage to
turn many abstract nouns into...
a substance that can be experienced,
maybe that day it will make sense that
you tell us about Christ and God.
                    —a revolutionary comrade,
                    cited by Hugo Assman

The Christian experience in revolutionary Nicaragua has its roots in what has become known as liberation theology.

The Second Vatican Council called by Pope John XXIII in 1962 prescribed a gospel-oriented content for Christianity and a more socially conscious doctrine than that of previous papal encyclicals. A general ecumenical opening-up allowed for dialogue with other denominations and with non-Christians. Lay people were given more responsibility in the pastoral work of the church. Liturgical reforms included the introduction of language, songs and instruments native to different cultures and an end to masses in which priests kept their back to the people.

In 1968 Vatican II found its Latin American application in the meeting of bishops in Medellin, Colombia. There the documents of Vatican II were interpreted in light of the dependent reality of the continent. The bishops declared that the people were oppressed by the "institutionalized violence" of internal and external colonial structures which "seeking unbounded profits, ferment an economic dictatorship and the international imperialism of money."

Medellin opened the way for the futher legitimization of what was already underway within the church throughout Latin America. In the mid-sixties, a group of Maryknoll nuns from the U.S. were expelled from Guatemala for "subversive activities". In Colombia, Father Camilo Torres, a commander in the guerrilla army, was killed in combat. The Christians for Socialism in Chile, the Third World Priests in Argentina and the ONIS movement in Peru and in Colombia are evidence, a few years later, of a growing movement. The heroic examples of revolutionary commitment by Christians are no longer isolated.

A spectre is haunting Latin America: it is liberation theology. It is a theology that returns to the origins of Christianity, is strongly rooted in Biblical experience and claims the historical role of Jesus the liberator. It recovers the true message of the word of God, distorted through centuries of domination. But, above all, liberation theology emerges from a practice of Christian faith in the daily lives of men and women whose need to live out their doctrines has led them to find new formulations for their faith. It is also a rediscovery of the ministry of each person in relation to the community or society. The sharing of the ministry, through an increased participation of lay people in the Christian community, means less religious ornamentation and a demystification of the role of the priest (or the bishop or the Pope). The emphasis is no longer on the hierarchical figure, but on the meaning and on the act of faith itself.

The Christian base communities were also part of the secularization of many church practices. Medellin had encouraged the establishment of these community organizations where Christians could join together in smaller numbers than the traditional parish structure. These communities continue to be the centre from which hundreds and thousands of Christian revolutionaries proclaim and develop their practice of faith. The Christian base communities are the organs whereby the poor who have never made decisions about their lives become self-determining human beings, no longer objects but subjects of history. In Brazil, for example, there are 80,000 such communities with approximately two million members. These are the only popular structures that have been able to continue intact after almost two decades of systematic repression.

Delegates of the Word, lay people trained in social promotion and to offer some of the church's rites, have been especially important in the Nicaraguan countryside where there is a scarcity of priests. Many women serve as delegates. Currently, in a huge area on the Atlantic Coast in Nicaragua, a movement to create Ministers of the Holy Supper has developed. Already there are more than twenty Delegates of the Word who have been given special training so that they can celebrate "the Lord's Supper" using local "bread and wine" (tortillas, chica, etc.) and a text that also originates out of the day-to-day lives of the people.

Is this a celebration of the Eucharist? Perhaps not, because these people are not priests, and do not have the authority that Rome confers on those who are. But with this practice one of the last exclusive fields of the clergy is being undermined. (I say "one of the last" because the last one will likely be the masculine monopoly of the Catholic ministry.)

Liberation theology pushes the church to become an institution of social criticism and to place itself at the service of the exploited and oppressed; a non-critical stance towards social injustice is an indication of an endorsement of inequitable, oppressive conditions. At the same time, liberation theology does not imply that the church should assume the mantle of leadership against oppression but that the institutional power of the church must support social action aimed at transforming this reality.

The church, like every other economic, political and social institution, is not outside history. It is part of history and takes place within it. Therefore it is not outside the class struggle that rules all areas of human life. The power in today's church is the power of capital. And as such, it is fighting desperately (just as capital is fighting in the class war of each country, and in its imperialist phase at the international level) in order to maintain its domination.

The enemies of change understand this very well. In May of 1980, during Ronald Reagan's election campaign, a group of "experts" associated with him and known as the Sante Fe Committee produced a document outlining his future policies. The Sante Fe Document touches upon all the aspects that make up the renewed plan for U.S. domination in Latin America. It states that "American foreign policy must begin to confront, and not merely react in a belated manner, to the liberation theology that is being used in Latin America by the 'theology of liberation' clergy."

This awareness of the importance and danger of the

committed church is not a new thing for imperialism. In the report presented to President Nixon by the Rockefeller Commission in 1969, we read:

Modern communications and an increase in education have caused an agitation among the people that has had a tremendous impact on the church, turning it into a fighting force committed to change — and if necessary, revolutionary change. . . In effect, the church could be in a similar position to that of young people — with a profound idealism but penetrated by subversion, ready to carry out a revolution if it is necessary in order to end injustice, but without clarity about the ultimate nature of the revolution itself or of the system of government through which the sought-for justice can be carried out.

It is significant that this report clearly admits that communication and education are primarily responsible for the fact that the people and the church are becoming aware of their situation and of the need to change it.

And the revolution — which has sometimes been slower to understand the world situation than the enemy — also begins to understand the logical and necessary collaboration between Christian commitment and the revolutionary struggle of oppressed peoples.

The church in Nicaragua

Every revolutionary process of
liberation is, for the believer,
a piece of the History of Salvation. . .
The moments of revolution are also
moments of Revelation.
                                    —Pablo Richard

Entre Christianismo y Revolution. . . No Hay Contradiccion! There is no contradiction between Christianity and Revolution! is a shout that goes up from the hearts of thousands of people, young and old, in churches, in the streets, in demonstrations and gatherings of all kinds. The church's place in history is being put to the test in Nicaragua. For centuries, powerful class interests succeeded in perverting the original teachings of Christ. Today the people are rebelling, inside as well as outside the church's still-feudal structure.

Christians played a central role in the anti-Somoza struggle. In the Christian base communities and among the rural population Christians suffered under the 50-year Somoza dictatorship. Christians rebelled because it was impossible to believe in a God of life and remain in a country where life was negated, to believe in justice and to live in the midst of injustice. Christians fought against the regime, defeating Somoza's system and laying the foundations for a new society in their homeland.

On July 19, 1979, almost a half century of struggle culminated in the overthrow of the repressive tyranny of Anastasio Somoza. It is impossible to understand the victory without knowing something about the conditions that the majority of Nicaraguans faced under Somoza. As in many other Latin American countries the most visible and brutal characteristic of life in Nicaragua was the contrast between the extreme poverty of the majority and the tremendous wealth of the very few.

Illiteracy was over 50 per cent and rose to more than 90 per cent in some rural areas. Unemployment was acute. Health care existed only for those living in the capital city who had money or political pull; there were many parts of the country that had never seen a doctor. In some areas, especially in the mining region and on the Atlantic Coast, tuberculosis was simply something "most people had." In many rural zones night blindness and endemic madness reached epidemic proportions as a result of widespread malnutrition. Statistics have shown the highest infant mortality rate in Latin America to be variably that of Brazil, Haiti and Nicaragua. If Nicaragua wasn't actually at the top of that tragic list, it was consistently one of the worst countries on the continent.

Misery in Nicaragua resulted not just from the grossly unfair distribution of goods, but was also a product of the reign of terror used to maintain the status quo. Sandino, the man who kicked the U.S. Marines out of Nicaragua in the mid-thirties, was called a bandit; history books ignored or distorted his role and mere possession of a picture of the national hero could mean death or imprisonment. As the struggle against Somoza developed, repression became more selective and more widespread at the same time. In the north, whole villages of peasants were tortured, murdered, the women raped and the men thrown from helicopters. Hundreds disappeared. In the prisons, the torture of political prisoners was a sport for those close to the dictator — and for the dictator himself.

Even in Nicaragua's early history there are examples of blood-thirsty Christianizers and also of the men whose approach involved a more just treatment of the native peoples. In some cases one can even speak of precursors to those who are now engaged in promoting a faith that better reflects the needs of human life. The friar Bartolome de las Casas, with his passionate defence of the natives, influenced not only Mexican history but that of Central America, including of course Nicaragua.

The Dominican bishop Fray Antonio de Valdivieso, the first true martyr in the Nicaraguan church, arrived in Leon in 1544 as the third bishop-elect in the country. He was in a way the precursor of El Salvador's Monsignor Oscar Arnulfo Romero, and his actions were prophetic of those of the present-day Christians for Socialism. Valdivieso, who was accompanied in his struggle to defend the Indians by the bishops of Chiapas and Guatemala, was assassinated by an agent of the Spanish crown on February 26, 1550.

As in every other country in the New World, the Catholicism brought from Spain was marked by the autonomous religiosity of the Nicaraguan native peoples.

In this way an eclecticism developed that combined indigenous myths, rites and feasts with the liturgy brought over by the conquerors. The peoples had patron saints and religious festivals that incorporated popular traditions in the development of Christian faith in the country.

In the early years of the twentieth century new religious orders took root in Nicaragua, strengthening the political and social influence of the church. Educational centres for the white bourgeoisie, and in some cases special schools or annexes for middle and low-income children, were founded. Among these orders the most important were the Salesians, the Christian Brothers, the Jesuits, the Dominicans, the Franciscans, Mothers of Mary the Helper, and the Josephines.

The hierarchy of the Catholic Church in general supported the Somoza dynasty until, swept up in the tremendous wave of popular struggle, it was forced to change its attitude in the 1960s. But even the church hierarchy had its patriots. Monsignor Calderon y Padilla of Matagalpa refused to attend the pontifical requiem mass for the soul of Somoza Garcia and went instead to do pastoral work in his diocese while the dictator's funeral was taking place. Calderon y Padilla became a focus of the anti-Somoza attitudes within the church hierarchy in the fifties and sixties; he supported the campaigns to release political prisoners and refused to participate in the clergy's legitimization of the regime.

The first contacts between the Christian movement and the FSLN took place in three main areas: between the Christian Youth Movement *(Movimiento Juveil Cristiano)* and the youth of the Revolutionary Student Front *(Frente Estudiantil Revolucionario)*; between the leaders of the FSLN and some priests and nuns who clearly identified with the people in struggle (among them Ernesto and Fernando Cardenal, Uriel Molina, Monsignor Jose Arias Caldera, Marta Frech and Maria Hartman); and in the rural areas, where the Delegates of the Word were emerging from the poorest sections of Nicaraguan peasantry. These contacts, and their implicatons for the future role of Christians in the revolution are described in this book.

These experiences are not separate from the general consciousness-raising movement among practicing and non-practicing Christians throughout those years, both in the church and in the overall political scene. Other examples of this new climate were: the first strike in Catholic schools; the confrontation in the Central American University; the positions taken by groups of priests such as the so-called "seven brothers in Marx"; the take overs of churches; the "journalism in the catacombs"; the letter from the Capuchin monks denouncing the genocide of over 350 peasants in the northern part of the country in June, 1976; the immense work done in the rural areas by members of the national team for pastoral work to form peasants' organizations; the June, 1979 Pastoral Letter from the bishops supporting armed struggle as a legitimate form of defeating the dictatorship; and also the extraordinary testimony given by the life of the priest and guerrilla commander Gaspar Garcia Laviana. His letter, written when he was about to join the guerrillas, was an example for the Nicaraguan people:

Day of the Nativity of our Savior.
December 25, 1977.
Somewhere in Nicaragua.

Nicaraguan brothers and sisters:
During these Christmas holidays, when we celebrate the birth of Christ, our Lord and Savior who came into the world to announce the kingdom of justice, I have decided to address you as my brothers in Christ to tell you of my decision to join the clandestine struggle as a soldier of the Lord and as a soldier of the Sandinista National Liberation Front.

I came to Nicaragua from my birth land, Spain, about nine years ago, as a missionary of the Sacred Heart. I gave myself passionately to the labors of preaching, and soon I began to discover that the oppressed and humilated people I was serving as a priest were hungry and thirsty for justice, and that this demanded the comfort of actions more than the comfort of words.

As an adoptive Nicaraguan and as a priest, I have seen the open wounds of my people. I have seen the shameful exploitation of the peasantry, crushed under the boot of the landowners, who are protected by a National Guard. I have seen a few grow obscenely rich in the shadow of the Somoza dictatorship. I have witnessed the degrading traffic in human flesh to which poor young women are subjected, forced into prostitution by the powerful. And I have touched with my own hands the baseness, the humiliation, the deceit and the robbery brought by the power and domination of the Somoza family.

Corruption and repression are merciless. They are deaf to words and will continue to be deaf, while my people groan in the dark night from the bayonets and my brothers suffer torture and prison for demanding a just and free nation, from which robbery and assassination are gone forever.

And because our honest youth, the best sons of Nicaragua, are at war against the oppressive tyranny, I have decided to join this war as the humblest soldier in the Sandinista Front. This is a just war, one which the holy gospels see as good and which my conscience as a Christian says is good, because it represents the struggle against a state of affairs that is hateful to the Lord our God. As the Medellin documents, signed by the bishops of Latin America, state in the chapter on the Latin American situation, "revolutionary insurrection can be legitimate in the case of a clear and persistent tyranny which gravely endangers fundamental human rights and greatly harms the common good of the nation, whether this tyranny originates in one individual or in clearly unjust structures."

To all my Nicaraguan brothers: I ask you, for the love of Christ, to support the struggle of the Sandinista Front, so that the day of redemption for our people may not be delayed any longer. And to those who through fear or necessity are still serving Somoza, especially the honest officers and soldiers of the National Guard, I say to you that you still have time to side with justice, which is to side with Our Lord.

To businessmen who have not taken part in the corruption, to the honest farmers, to the professionals and technicians who reject the chaos and despotism that Somoza represents, I tell you that for each one of you there is a place beside the Sandinista Front, to bring dignity to our people.

To my brothers the workers on plantations and in workshops, to the artisans, to the forgotten ones who have no roof and no work and live in marginal slums, to my peasant brothers, to those who work in the harvest, crowded in camps, to the cane-cutters and day-laborers, to all those who have been robbed of opportunities in this land, I say to you it is time to close ranks around the Sandinista Front, to join our hands and our arms, because the sound of the guns of justice in our mountains, towns and villages is the sign of the redemption drawing near. With the rebellion of us all, the insurrection that we will all bring about, the darkness of Somoza will give way to light.

To my brothers who are fighting with the Sandinista Front on the Northern Carlos Fonseca Amador Front, in the northeastern Pablo Ubeda Front, in the southern Benjamin Zeledon Front, and in the centres for urban resistance, I tell you my firm conviction that the day of victory will be built by the sacrifice of our fallen heroes, who embody our people's will to fight by the revolutionary dedication of the people itself, organized for struggle and by the sacrifice we are ready to make in the trenches, united around the National Directorate.

The Somoza system is a sin, and to free ourselves from oppression is to free us from sin. With my gun in my hand, full of faith and love for my Nicaraguan people, I will fight to my last breath for the coming of the kingdom of justice in our homeland, that kingdom of justice that the Messiah announced to us under the light of the star of Bethlehem.

> *Your brother in Christ,*
> *Patria Libre O Morir**
> *Gaspar Garcia Laviana*
> *Missionary priest of the Sacred Heart*

The great majority of Christian revolutionaries are not Marxists; their understanding of reality does not come from an ideology which they have studied or which "has been imported," but rather from consciously analyzing what surrounds them. One of the elements that permitted and in fact encouraged collaboration among revolutionaries, Christians and non-Christians, was the trust born from years of living and working together. One after another, the testimonies gathered here reflect this.

The FSLN, leadership of the revolutionary struggle in Nicaragua, has in its ranks both revolutionary Christians and revolutionaries who are not Christians. Together they resurrected the teachings and the courage of Augusto C. Sandino; together they carried out a relentless struggle that covered twenty years of national history. They fought, died together, gave up almost everything, and won.

We told Commander Fidel Castro, when he came to Nicaragua, that here we do not have a purely strategic alliance, but rather a unity, a unity forged in the very heart of the struggle.
—Father Uriel Molina

But what has happened since the victory? The very first thing to consider is the position of the Sandinista Popular Revolution with respect to religion. This position has been very clear from the first days of the struggle, and is also

*Free Homeland or Death

evident in the Christian background of many of its leaders. We have yet to see a single event that could be interpreted as repression against the church. The FSLN's position is outlined in detail in the important Document of the National Directorate of the FSLN on Religion, which deserves to be quoted in full.

For the FSLN, the freedom to practice a religious faith is an inalienable human right which is fully guaranteed by the revolutionary government. This principle has been part of our revolutionary program for a long time, and we will continue to give it effective support in the future.

We the Sandinistas affirm that our experience shows that when Christians, basing themselves on their faith, are able to respond to the needs of the people and the needs of history, their own beliefs lead them towards revolutionary militancy. Our experience shows that one can be at once a believer and a consistent revolutionary, and that there is no insuperable contradiction between these two states.

Outside the framework of the party, Christian militants, be they priests, pastors, nuns or lay people, have every right to express their convictions in public, without in the least affecting their militance within the FSLN or the confidence they have earned through their revolutionary work.

The FSLN has a deep respect for all our people's religious celebrations and traditions and is making efforts to recuperate the true meaning of these celebrations, attacking the vices and manifestations of corruption associated with these in the past. We believe that this respect must be shown not only by guaranteeing the conditions in which these traditions may express themselves fully, but also by not using these celebrations for partisan or commercial purposes.

No Sandinista militant, as such, ought to pass judgment on religious questions whose interpretation belongs to the different churches. These questions must be publicized by Christians among themselves. If a Sandinista who is also a

Christian intervenes in the debates that arise on such occasions, he or she does this individually and in his or her role as a Christian.

Some ideologues of reaction have accused the FSLN of attempting to divide the church. This accusation is completely false and insidious.

If there are divisions within religion, this is a fact completely independent of the will and actions of the FSLN.

In the present stage, this situation continues. There is a vast majority of Christians which supports and actively takes part in the revolution. Logically, the Sandinistas are good friends of revolutionary Christians but not with counter-revolutionaries, even when they call themselves Christians.

The revolutionary state, like every modern state, is a secular state and cannot adopt any religion, because it represents all the people, both believers and non-believers.

The National Directorate of the Sandinista National Liberation Front, in issuing this official communique, wants not only to clarify the topic at hand but also, and mainly, to allow all the revolutionaries active in the FSLN and in the churches to see the duties and responsibilities that they bear, in this country devasted by 159 years of pillage, repression and dependence. To build the future of Nicaragua is a historical challenge that goes beyond our borders, and encourages other peoples who are struggling for their liberation and for the development of new human beings; this is the right and duty of all Nicaraguans, regardless of religious beliefs.

This is not merely a case of a revolution that acknowledges and respects freedom of worship. It is a revolution that was won by Christians as well as by non-Christians. The list of priests and religious people who occupy posts at all levels of government, who are in charge of schools and hospitals, and who serve the people on the Council of State and in other posts of responsibility, would be too long to include here.

Powerful sectors of the Nicaraguan church hierarchy have done everything possible to get those in top government posts to resign. On May 13, 1980 the bishops declared, "We believe that, since the exceptional circumstances are no longer in effect, lay Christians can fulfil the public duties now being carried out by some priests in a no less efficient manner."

At about this time, I witnessed a baptism celebrated by one of these priests. He explained the origin and meaning of the ceremony, applying the reinterpretation of liberation theology. "We now know," he said, "that original sin consists of society's division into classes...Let all selfishness, capitalism, Somozism, go out of this girl!" He finished by saying, as he touched the little girl's forehead with water, "Now I give you your revolutionary militancy."

It is not difficult to understand why the bishops want to refuse revolutionary priests the possibility of continuing to function as ministers of the sacraments. What could be a more meaningful, or more profound interpretation of baptism in today's Nicaragua?

The attempt to drive the priests in the government out of their posts is not the only effort to discredit the revolutionary process. During the Somoza regime the bishops did not insist on the separation of church and state; on the contrary, the priests who acted as chaplains to the National Guard were never questioned, except by the people themselves. But since the popular victory of July 19, Obando y Bravo (the archbishop of Managua) has been carrying out a systematic campaign that includes removing almost every single priest and nun who openly identifies with the people.

It is clear that reactionary elements in the church want to cause a rupture between the church and the revolution. The hierarchy of the church feels threatened and is trying to make it seem as if the Christian faith is being suppressed by the revolution. It may be the only case in history in which the hierarchical church is repressing the revolutionary church in a context where the people are in power.

The Pope's visit to Nicaragua in March, 1983 brought these contradictions to the fore. After an on-again off-again "courting" period, the Pope finally announced that he would arrive in Nicaragua the morning of March 4. We knew that the Pope was coming to give the Nicaraguan reactionary bishops a shot in the arm, to criticize the "priests in government" and to bolster the counter-revolution. But we had no idea it would be as bad as it was.

Everything was suddenly compounded by the fact that the day before the Pope's visit there was a mass burial of seventeen young Sandinistas—members of the youth movement who had been in the reserve batallions in the north and were ambushed in the mountains of Matagalpa. Seventeen young men, barely more than children, who died singing because their ammunition gave out after seven hours of combat. We bade them farewell at the military academy on the hill and carried their coffins to the huge July 19 Plaza, where thousands came in rage and tears.

The next day, beginning with the Pope's initial address to the government and people at the airport, it was clear that he had come to lecture and not to listen. After the formal speeches, the Pope made his way along the reception line to the strains of the "peasant mass," music deeply loved by Nicaraguan Christians but outlawed in several of the country's dioceses by Obando y Bravo's Episcopal Conference.

Father Ernesto Cardenal, poet and minister of culture, was on the reception line with his cabinet colleagues. When John Paul came to where he stood, a short exchange took place. Journalists positioned some distance away immediately had a variety of interpretations for what had taken place. Ernesto fell to his knees and tried to kiss the Pope's hand. What the head of the Roman Catholic Church had said was, "You'd better put your relationship with the church in order."

After the airport ceremony, a helicopter took His Holiness to Leon, the second largest city in the country. There the subject of the Pope's address was education, and he failed to mention Nicaragua's extraordinary literacy crusade which, in 1980, reduced the country's illiteracy rate from 53 per cent to just over 12 per cent of the population.

The day culminated in Managua with an outdoor mass in the July 19 Plaza, an event attended by an estimated 800,000 people (one-fifth of the country's population). The day before, 10,000 people had gathered in the same square to pay tribute to the young Sandinistas who had died in battle. Now, during the Pope's mass, their families and friends wanted the Pope to understand what was happening in Nicaragua, to feel their pain, to sympathize with their desire for a principled peace. But he refused. The mothers of the most recent victims, standing up front, held photos of their sons for the Pope to see. But all they received was his angry "Silence..." His inappropriate sermon was then increasingly interrupted by the people shouting "PEOPLE'S POWER...PEOPLE'S POWER ...PEOPLE'S POWER."

Pope John Paul II had the opportunity in Nicaragua to open his eyes and ears. He was given the unique chance of understanding the reality of a country whose deeply Catholic people are following Christ's message in their daily lives. He chose neither to see nor to hear.

Revolutionary Christians in Nicaragua insist that their aim is not to divide the church. They recognize the authority of the bishops and of the Pope, and have remained loyal to them. But their actions alongside the people also reflect another loyalty—to the Word of God, to the church itself, to Christ and to their people. They assert that it is in the name of this loyalty that they identify with and serve a people that is liberating itself. They also hold that there is no contradiction between the doctrines of their faith and those of the revolutionary process. And further, they believe that the Sandinista Popular

Revolution verifies and confirms the search for God in our lives.

When they are asked whether there are one or two churches in Nicaragua, or if one can see a split within the church, the majority of Christians insist that there is only one church, and they sharply reject the notion of a division. Only one of the many priests with whom I have spoken on this subject talks about the possibility of a schism similar to that suffered by the church 400 years ago. Faced with the deep differences between the two positions found in the church today, this man of faith mentions this possibility, although he affirms "this is not what we want."

The official church does recognize the existence of class struggle. The "Pastoral Message of the Nicaraguan Bishops" signed by the bishops in November, 1979 states:

. . . in respect to the struggle between social classes, we believe that there is a difference between the dynamic fact of a class struggle that leads to a just transformation of the structures, and on the other hand the class hatred that is directed against individuals and is in radical opposition to the Christian duty of governing according to love.

At the present time, at least, the practice of the majority of the bishops does not correspond to the awareness embodied in this message.

In Nicaragua "the dice have been thrown." The everyday reality of Christians and non-Christians working together for a more just and humane society wreaks havoc on the stereotyped images of socialism or communism as the "antichrist." On an almost totally Christian continent, the example set by Nicaraguan Christians is one that imperialism cannot tolerate.

The Vatican itself is concerned about a situation that is getting out of hand. Among other repressive moves, it has issued a decree (going into effect this coming November) forcing the hundreds of orders of nuns back into their convents, into the medieval habits many of them have shed, and back under the control of their bishops. (Not too many years ago, the women of the church were not taken seriously; today they have shown themselves to be—as is also true outside the church—a revolution within a revolution.)

The next few years will undoubtedly bring new struggles and further the development of irreversible trends within the church. For, as can clearly be seen in Nicaragua, there is no contradiction between true Christianity and people's revolution...but between the people and their oppressors within or outside the church, the contradiction is irreconcilable.

Here then is the story of Solentiname, the story of Riguero...stories intimately linked to the history of Christian participation in Nicaragua's struggle for liberation, and linked—as well—to the history of a revolutionary vanguard engaged in an armed struggle that found a source of great strength, commitment and leadership from among masses of Christian brothers and sisters. The testimonies were gathered in Nicaragua throughout 1981 and 1982. Those involved gave generously of their time and memories. This is not "past history" but very much in the present, and the struggle taking place in this context has profound meaning not only for Nicaragua, but for Latin America...and the world. The full implications of this struggle will perhaps only be complete as time goes by. For now, we give the floor to those who searched for changes in their lives and in their society.

Part I: Solentiname

Solentiname

*T*he voices you will hear in the following pages belong to those who took an island and a dream into their own hands, back in 1966. Solentiname: an archipelago of 38 small islands in Lake Nicaragua, near the Costa Rican shore. Solentiname: from 1966 to 1977, a place known throughout the world for the presence, on one of its islands, of a priest-poet who drew attention to its name, tragedy, and beauty. It has been as well-known for its part in an important movement, that of the Christians in the Nicaraguan revolutionary struggle. Solentiname was a monastry, a workshop for artists, a meeting place for poets, a commune and a military training school.

Ernesto Cardenal, poet and priest (and now minister of culture) left his wealthy family after important reflections at the abbey of Gethsemani (Kentucky), in Mexico and in Colombia, and arrived in this corner of the country, in this space filled with misery and need.

William Agudelo, a Columbian youth, student at the Medellin seminary, met Ernesto in Medellin and decided to go with him to Solentiname. Today, his considerable talents as a graphic designer and singer are at the service of his adopted homeland.

Olivia Silva, a peasant woman from the Solentiname islands, was one of the first local people to receive the pioneers, at the very inception of the community. Today she lives in Managua, painting and teaching painting in workshops. **Natalia Sequeira,** Olivia's close friend and the unofficial doctor of that remote community, was another loyal member of this exceptional group. Both are mothers of patriots who fell so their homeland could be reborn.

Oscar Mairena, Alejandro Guevara, Nubia Arcia, Manuel Alvarado and **Teresita Builes** are the young people of the community. Oscar is still in the countryside, working on the land with his wife and children. Alejandro stayed in the Sandinista People's Army after the revolutionary victory. Today, he is a captain in the region around Rio San Juan and administers the new community that is rising from the ashes of the previous one.

Nubia is Alejandro's wife. She was a teacher, the first that the children of Solentiname ever had. Now she lives with her own children — and with Alejandro, when his work allows it — as a permanent resident of the community. She administers as well, but also organizes and dreams. Manuel Alvarado, a peasant from the islands, also stayed. He works with all that grows.

Teresita Builes is William's wife. As the first woman to live in the community she changed its "monastic" atmosphere. Teresita, William and their three children now live in Managua.

We will hear from Ernesto, William, Olivia, Natalia, Oscar, Alejandro, Nubia, Manuel and Teresita. They tell us their story, the story of Solentiname — an important part of the history of the Christian communities in the process of struggle in Nicaragua, an important part of the struggle in Nicaragua, an important part of Nicaragua itself.

The first rule is, there won't be any rules

Ernesto Cardenal: I was ordained as a priest to come and establish the community here. It was Thomas Merton who gave me the idea. He had been a monk for twenty years and had written a great deal about that life but had become unhappy with monastic life. He was a famous contemplative writer, and during the early 1960s many young Americans went into Trappist monasteries because of him. Monasteries were multiplying in the U.S., in part because of Thomas Merton's books. And after twenty years, Merton was wanting out...

He knew it was a medieval, anachronistic lifestyle. Ridiculous. So he wanted to found a different kind of contemplative community outside the U.S. Merton was an enemy of the U.S., of Yankee civilization and everything it represented. He hated the bourgeois mentality most monks had. Despite being monks, they had reactionary politics. At first it was a shock for me to find out that he wanted to leave the life I was still so enthusiastic about. He told me that I was in my monastic honeymoon and that within a few years I too would find the life arid.

He thought this new community should be in Latin America. He wanted it to be in a poor place, with a peasant population, maybe with Indians. The original idea was to build it in the Andes. He talked about Ecuador, Colombia, Peru. So I said to him, why not Nicaragua? That's when he began to think seriously about the possiblity of Nicaragua. First we considered the Rio San Juan province. Coronel Urtecho,* to whom I wrote, persuaded us not to go there because of the climate. You couldn't grow anything. Besides, the mosquitoes and the daily rain...Another possibility was the island of Ometepe. Merton went through the paperwork with his superiors in Rome, or rather with the Vatican itself, so he could leave the congregation.

---

*Jose Coronel Urtecho, a great Nicaraguan poet who lives close by the San Juan River.

At first he had thought about a monastery in Latin America, a sort of reformed Trappist Order, for instance not wearing the habits. He wrote to Pope John XXIII who replied that he thought all Merton's suggestions were good, but that they should be implemented by a different order, not the Trappists. The Trappists should remain as it had been founded in the thirteenth century and innovations should be made by other orders. Merton read me the letter, and said, "the Pope is quite right. But what I want to do is leave here and found this new order."

Actually, his abbot went to Rome and convinced them not to allow him to leave. I imagine that the main reason was that he would create traumas for many youths, and for priests already trained by him. And he also made a lot of money for the monastery with his books.

I was the only novice he let know about the plan. He also told two other monks about it. He thought that the four of us would be the only ones to leave.

Next, I got sick. I had a continuous headache. They gave me all kinds of treatments but couldn't find a cure and after a while I couldn't keep up my responsibilities. I had to be exempted from more and more things: my work, choir, etc. And then a monk who had been a doctor before, and who was one of the ones involved in plans for the new monastery, said that I had to leave. For me this was a great shock. I went to see Merton almost in tears.

He cheered me up right away, and said it was a good thing. I was two months away from taking my vows. "But that's why it's a good thing. If you leave before making your vows then you won't have the problem I do being a monk from the Trappist order. We are planning to leave anyway, now you can leave early."

Shortly after that an abbot from Cuernavaca came to visit. He was a good friend of Merton through correspondence. He was establishing a monastery which was quite progressive. This was before Vatican II. Both Merton and the abbot, Father Lemercier, had progressive ideas, which afterwards influenced the Vatican Council and the whole church...Merton spoke to him about my case. He said I could be accepted into his monastery as either a monk or a guest. I didn't want to go there as a monk so I went to Mexico as a guest.

In the meantime, Merton suggested I begin to study for the priesthood. The church was still very clerical, so it would be important to be a priest in the kind of community we had in mind — especially if Merton was not allowed to leave and I had to establish the community. It would be difficult to exercise spiritual leadership if I wasn't a priest.

I studied for two years in Cuernavaca. While I was there Merton notified me that he had been denied permission to leave Gethsemani. He also informed us that he had been forbidden to write so that letter would be his last. It was quite a shock. We had already made plans for his arrival in Mexico; his previous letters even dealt with the clothes he was going to wear when he arrived. He didn't want to dress in black like the Jehovah's Witnesses. He was going to come dressed as a sort of student...we had everything ready. The plan was for him to stay in Mexico for about two months and then to go and find a place for the new community.

After his last letter, I continued my studies as he had advised me. Then bit by bit we started up a clandestine correspondence. At first he would send poems with a short note inside. Then letters. In special circumstances monks can write sealed letters which the abbot cannot read. But as this exception became rather frequent, the abbot complained. Eventually the correspondence became normal again, although we still wrote in a kind of code. For example, the plan for the community was known as Ometepe, after the place that we had chosen. The abbot didn't know our meaning of Ometepe.

I finished my studies for the priesthood in Colombia.

William Agudelo: I already knew Ernesto. In 1964, the year I came to the seminary, Ernesto had been at

Gethsemani as a novice monk and was beginning seminary studies to become a priest. I knew of him as a Nicaraguan poet, as someone who understood art and painting. I like to draw very much so I was very interested in making contact with him. But I was scared to approach him. I was very shy — I still am — and I couldn't imagine our having a close relationship. I actually met him through a friend. I was writing a diary, and my friend who had read part of it and who was in contact with Ernesto told Ernesto about me. At that time Ernesto was in charge of the workshop we were attending, a seminar to learn to appreciate painting and art and to learn art history.

The connection began there. Getting to know him changed the direction of my life. When I met him I was faced with the dilemma of whether to stay in the seminary or not. I was inclined toward leaving, but still had doubts. He was very helpful. He helped me find a way to resolve this dilemma and also validated my need to make time to write. When that year ended — Solentiname was still a beautiful mystery, a deep, almost invisible thing — and after I left the seminary I went to visit Ernesto quite regularly. I spoke with him. We discussed what I was writing. I asked for his advice... I was already writing poetry. He was very enthusiastic. Ernesto communicates this enthusiasm. I know very few people like him. Really, when he discovers any talent at all he gets excited about it. It's as if he himself were creating. And he plunges right into it, and there is no time limit, he spends hours with you talking about the stuff, making you see things.

It was clear I was not going to be a priest, but I had a longing for the contemplative life, just like Ernesto. Til then it seemed that if you wanted to develop yourself in the contemplative life, you had to go into a monastery where the first thing they do, or they used to do, if you were an artist, was to clamp down on that. Ernesto is a poet and had been in the monastery, he could describe it to you: a painter would come, or a sculptor, and they would prohibit their work.

Ernesto had already spoken with Thomas Merton and had plans for a community of people who would not be priests exactly, but wanted a contemplative religious life and the chance to develop themselves as artists. Solentiname came to fulfil that vision. The idea was to go and live in a beautiful place, with peasants. A place where you can grow in contemplation, but also have time to write, to develop as an artist.

In 1965 Ernesto suggested I go with him. I was very enthused of course. But the problem was my personal life. There weren't going to be any women there, it would be like a monastery, in practice it *was* a monastery. Women were not supposed to even visit. This question was not resolved for me since by that time I had a fairly advanced, serious and intense relationship with Teresita.

Ernesto: Real life, together with the training I had received from Merton, was leading me in a new direction. He had spoken to me from the beginning about what he wanted to do. That it would have to be without habits, and without the formalities of monasteries; we'd lead a normal, simple life in the countryside. He told me that this was how the first contemplative people who retired to the desert lived. They did not want to remain in Rome living in an unjust society. He said we should try to live in contact with nature, with the peasants, and with God. That contemplative life was not so different from the other life; it was simply life.

After I was ordained as a priest I went to visit Merton once more. I went to Kentucky to ask him for more concrete orientation. One of the first things I asked was his help in elaborating the rules we would have. He said, "The first rule will be that there won't be any rules. So all the other rules are redundant."

I accepted the idea that there weren't going to be any rules. Still I asked him, should we not smoke? And he answered, "Why not? Why not do it? Really, I have no reason. It's bad for your health, because it has been

proven to cause cancer, and besides it's very expensive,"
he said. "But I don't see why you shouldn't smoke there."

It was our guardian angel who came to Solentiname

Ernesto: When I was ordained I already knew I'd be
coming here, that I wouldn't be sent as a parish priest
somewhere else... I had visited Solentiname and knew it
was the right place. I arranged with a Bishop from this
area to allow me to establish an order here. As soon as I
was ordained, I came to San Carlos as an assistant to the
parish priest in the village while I looked for land in
Solentiname. Then Jose Coronel's wife, Maria Kautz, told
me that there was an old man, a big landowner who was
selling one of his lands. When we came to see it, we got off
the boat right here, on this point, and walked all around
here and finally arrived at the church.

I hadn't known beforehand that the church of
Solentiname was on his land. It was only half built and
made of adobe. Later we covered and painted it, leaving
the dirt floor. It seemed to me something... well, a very
special coincidence. I was not looking for a church, but
rather for the land, but on the land was the church of
Solentiname. And besides, walking near the church you
have the lake on both sides.

All this was wooded. It was like a jungle. You couldn't
see much. The whole area is equivalent to about 100 square
blocks. It was a very beautiful location, and I bought the
land. The owner had a debt with the bank, and I simply
took over the debt. It was 13,000 *cordobas*, which was
about 2,000 dollars. I had half from a literary prize I had
won, and I got the other half through collections among
friends in Managua.

In Colombia I had talked about the plan with some
friends who shared my ideas. Two of them left the
seminary and the priesthood in order to come with me.

Many of them did not believe it. Lots of people thought it was a lie that a priest was coming to Solentiname. When there weren't any priests in so many other places in Nicaragua, why would a priest come to Solentiname?

Olivia Silva: For me it was marvelous, it was like a miracle. I first heard that he was coming in June or July of 1965. An Italian priest from San Carlos came to Solentiname and he gave us the news. At first I didn't believe him. Such a sad, remote, abandoned place as Solentiname. It seemed absurd, a lie. But he was a priest so I took it seriously.

That was the year my oldest daughter was going to be married. If I had known that Ernesto was coming...but I didn't even know who Ernesto was, I'd never heard of him. We always went to the church, always. I was religious, so I would go and do the Stations of the Cross, the nine days for the Immaculate Conception, the month of the Sacred Heart of Jesus, the month of Mary. We would celebrate all that in church. But of course, as a personal initiative.

In spite of my doubts, Ernesto arrived in 1966. For us it was marvelous, a change in our life, a transformation in Solentiname. To be honest with you, well, it was our own guardian angel who had come to Solentiname.

We lived from agriculture. Or we half lived, because at that time agriculture didn't give you enough to live, barely to survive. There were many blights, there are still many blights in Solentiname. We always lived in continual work, and in poverty. You couldn't have any luxuries. Every year we would plant the beans, lots of them, and anything over and above what was needed for food, we would save for a radio. And we weren't able to buy it, ever.

Our plan was to build a new house. We didn't know how we would do it, but we had the idea. We lived in a very cold, freezing area and only had a dirt-floor house. The dampness affected my asthma. So we decided, with my oldest son Alejandro, to build a better house. But I couldn't see how. I've always said it was like a miracle, because we didn't have the wherewithal. How would we build that house? Impossible.

One Sunday morning we were clearing away stones on the point of the island when the boat Ernesto was in went by. The man who sold the land to Ernesto knew us and said, "Here's the little priest we're bringing you." That was on February 13.

Everybody welcomed him affectionately. Right away I saw the humility in that man. Priests would sometimes come by our island, priests who might be good characters and everything, but not with Ernesto's humility. I saw that he was such a simple little priest. I didn't think he was as intelligent as he is, being such a humble priest.

Natalia Sequeira: Ernesto came with Julio Centeno. Julio had told me he'd be coming on such and such a day with a priest who would buy his property and live here. And I said, oh Mr. Julio, how happy that would make us. We would have a priest. I told the other women and we all came to see him when he arrived. That day we heard mass.

We women were so happy. We were isolated without a priest. No priest came anymore to say mass. The church was closed, full of undergrowth, the statues, everything was abandoned there. We were so happy. We even had communion with him, all the women and Olivia's daughters. Olivia wasn't there because she was sick. I used to go to her place and massage her and give her injections. She had asthma. I was their doctor then.

Ernesto arrived to stay on a Sunday, the day after my daughter died. She was a year old when she died of hepatitis, in San Carlos. I had eleven children, all of them sick; you know the difficulties here, isolated, without a doctor. One would have to go all night on a boat, with your man on that little boat and you with your sick child. Instead of getting better the child would get worse. The difficulties. Olivia came over to tell me about Ernesto's arrival. *"Comadre"** she said, "the priest just went by; let's go, *comadre*, and have a good time," she said. "Let's go. Don't stay here crying, let's go to the church."

And so we went. They made their home in the church, arranged it, found a girl who would cook food for them and for their *companeros*. William was there, and Carlos Alberto, who later left. And another boy was with them. They lived in the church and together they began to build their little home.

The church was in bad shape, and when Ernesto came he started to rebuild it. If he hadn't come the church would have fallen down. That was their first home, the church. It was full of bush, you couldn't even see it. Since no priests came, no one used it. People hadn't wanted to do the clearing. They said, "What for? There isn't even a priest." Ernesto and his companions began to clear the under-growth, and looked for people to help with the cleaning.

Oscar Mairena: I was 19. I hadn't been in this area for too long when the poet came. It was a happy occasion when we found out a priest was coming. The community, all the people in Solentiname, were very happy. We received him well because this was an abandoned place, these islands. He wanted to meet the community, and soon began to call on us. We began to know each other better when we took part in the mass.

---

*Throughout this narrative Olivia and Natalia refer to each other as *"comadre,"* a term used in Latin America to refer to women who have baptized each other's children. It is derived from *madre*, mother. The literal translation is godmother, but this is a role which in Latin America has much more responsibility and social significance than we are familiar with in North America where it is almost entirely ceremonial.

The religious life we brought was quite different from what they were used to

Olivia: Social life, none. It was a neglected life. The people were traditionalist, poor, only peasants. There was a solidarity among the families, and a lot of camaraderie among the women. When one woman was going to give birth another one would be with her. The women did not smoke or drink. The woman who had a bit of food would help out another who didn't have anything, even in poverty. This is how we were. When I was growing up, and after I got married, there was still no school here.

Ernesto: Olivia and Natalia have told me that sometimes they ate only rice and beans and fish. Her children got to the point where they couldn't eat fish anymore. They got the cooking fat from the pig for frying. But they would run out and then they had to eat all their food boiled: boiled beans, boiled rice, boiled fish.

Alejandro Guevara: People ate the rice like that, but they didn't like beans just boiled and without salt, *sancochado*, as they called it. We have something against beans without salt here because we had to eat it all the time. There was no *corona* oil like we have now.

Ernesto: Alejandro's father, Julio Guevara, was the patriarch of Solentiname, the most respected old man, although he can't read.

Alejandro: He is honest, completely honest, and very kind. He is just like his own father who was one of the founders of Solentiname. He had a lot of land but he gave away his wood, gave away everything. Now he doesn't have so much.

Ernesto: When Alejandro's grandfather came there were

no people in Solentiname. There had been an indigenous population in pre-Columbian times — you can see that from the marvelous works of art — and afterwards the Guatuso Indians, a tribe that is becoming extinct in Costa Rica. We don't know why the Guatusos left Solentiname, since the soil was good. But the fact is that a century ago, when his grandfather came, there was nobody.

Alejandro: We grew up and then started to make our way back. At that time children went to Granada for school. My sister was educated there. After finishing school they returned to Solentiname. We had relatives in Granada, the Solarios, on our father's side. They are now the shame of the whole family. It turned out that Col. Solario was the interim chief of police at the time of the victory; they were Somoza people.

Ernesto: To go to Granada you had to go first to San Carlos in a rowboat; it would take hours of rowing to get there. And from there it would take another 18 or even 24 hours of rowing to reach Granada. Olivia talks about how hard those trips to San Carlos were for them; they'd go maybe once a week to sell their products. It took seven hours just one way, and then the trip back.

Alejandro: My childhood was just like that of any other child in Solentiname. The peasant father says: this child has to work, to help out. Once the child can work, they measure how much brush you can cut, and work you according to your strength. As far as school goes, I barely finished three grades, perhaps less.

Olivia: There was always a church, a little church that a man donated his house for. A priest called Andres Oviedo baptized almost all of our family in that little chapel. The priest used to come once a year or every eight months, to celebrate the Immaculate Conception or Saint Joseph.

Alejandro: The priest from San Carlos would come every six months to celebrate mass. One of them was called Chacon; he was dynamic but very reactionary. He would always charge to cover his costs. He would charge 200 or 300 *pesos* for mass. He also charged for baptisms. And when we celebrated Saint Joseph he would say that it was his saint's day and that it should be special, so he charged extra, the damned creep.

Father Chacon was a National Guard chaplain. He would scold the peasants. The whole sermon was just scolding. He was a Somocista. When Pedro Joaquin* was put in jail he said, "Pedro Joaquin, such a lively, intelligent boy, in jail for being an idiot!"

Natalia: Before this church was used there was another one, a little futher away and when a priest came we would go there. At least we could be happy for a couple of days. The priest would come for a few days and afterwards he'd leave. Sometimes we would celebrate the feast of Saint Joseph. Then more people would come from San Carlos and we'd have a festival. Later this church was started but was left half-finished. There might have been four of us wanting to fix it up but we didn't have any resources. No one else was interested.

Alejandro: Chacon yelled at everybody. His sermons would make a good novel; I knew them all, because at that time I wanted to be a priest. My mother, who had a typical Granada mentality, very Christian, thought that her brightest son should be a priest and brought me up thinking that. Until Ernesto took my vocation away.

Ernesto: I did not take it away. He continued like a priest, always.

*Pedro Joaquin Chamorro, leader of the anti-Somoza bourgeosie and editor of *La Prensa* newspaper, was imprisoned a number of times for his political activities during the Somoza regime, and finally murdered by the Somoza's on January 10, 1978.

Alejandro: My great desire was to be a priest; I didn't want to be anything else. As a traditional Christian, I wanted to live a really clean, saintly, and human life. And I had all the requirements. Especially when I realized you could be a saintly man, and someone with culture. That's the ideal...

This group of islands has been a very poor place, with all the consequences of poverty, including ignorance. The other day I was remembering that when there wasn't enough rain and the crops were drying out, the women would take a statue of the Virgin Mary and go around the island on a row boat or on foot singing so that it would rain. I was a kid and would go on those processions with the women. I believed in all that.

One day the women and girls were going around with a Madonna, singing so that it would rain, or it might have been so that it would stop raining; it had to be one or the other. And they passed under some trees. A kind of wasp nested in the trees and the noise the women made got the wasps in an uproar. It was terrible; the poor women were half-naked.

I also remember something else. In June you always had — everywhere in the country — a procession for the month of the Sacred Heart of Jesus. All the men would contribute five *pesos* and come to the church with candles to pray to the Heart of Jesus. The man who had the most money would buy gasoline for the outboard motor that we had on the island (there was only one); gasoline was about one *peso* for a gallon so it was quite a luxery. He would borrow the motor, buy a lot of *chicha** and come to sing to the Sacred Heart. The women would do the same for the Daughters of Mary, but that was in May.

Nubia Arcia: My childhood was much like Alejandro's. There isn't much difference between San Carlos and Solentiname. It's another backward village. I grew up just like that. My mother sent me to church, and my first communion was quite elaborate, with the fancy white

*A corn liquor.

dress and all that.

Even when I was in teachers' school, they made it compulsory to go to mass every Sunday. We also kept the first Friday of the month and said the rosary every day...But instead of becoming more religious I began rejecting all that. I would come back here on holidays and never go to church. But as a little girl, I dreamed about being a nun, the way Alejandro wanted to be a priest.

Ernesto: The religious life we brought was quite different from what they were used to.

Manuel Alvarado: When I went to Granada as a kid, my sister put me into the Legion of Mary. I went to study in the cathedral, to learn to be an altar boy, etc. They taught me the rosary. I even learned the rosary that you say for the dead. If anyone died, they sent for me to say the prayers you say nine days after death.

The people here really liked me to teach them the rosary for the dead; I had to mention the name of the dead person, because they said that if I didn't say their name, then the prayers were not going to reach God, because He wouldn't know who it was for. So I had to say, "these prayers are for the soul of so-and-so, who died." Even when Ernesto came here, I still kept on with this system of religion. I came here to celebrate mass with him.

Olivia: Nicaragua has been very tradition-bound, and this sort of religion is very deeply ingrained. That was the first thing our mothers did. I even brought my children up that way, with that fear.

I was a child like so many others in Nicaragua. My mother was a poor peasant, my father too. And they went to live in Solentiname where they brought up a large family of fourteen children. I am the sixth child; not one of the first but still one of the older ones. My father was off on his own so my mother was both the woman and man around the house. All of us children were very close to her;

she was a very loving mother. She brought us up and we stuck to her. Our home atmosphere was poor, but very religious.

Daughters never think badly of their mothers, and in fact my mother was an intelligent woman. She sewed artificial flowers and sold them very cheap, ten cents each. I helped her make those flowers so that we could survive. We sold them in December, the month we most looked forward to, because of the Nicaraguan tradition of the *Purisimas*.*

My husband and I were neighbors. You grow up and see things, and there comes a time when you have to fall in love, and so you do. I was about 20 and he was 34, much older than me. We had some children first and then got married when the priest came on his yearly visit. Of course you married for fear of being damned, because those who just lived together were damned. The biggest fear was that you wouldn't be able to be together when you died.

In fact, it was all those fears that helped us to change, to see that we couldn't stay with false rituals; that we had to change them to the reality that Jesus Christ wanted. Because I am telling you, I was very religious and I didn't have any problems understanding the revolution. I saw that the religion they gave us was alienating, it was not the reality of the Bible. I had studied the Bible with my oldest daughter and we always understood things differently than what the priests said. But when Ernesto came here I saw that we were understanding the Bible better than the priest. And we came to understand the revolution.

I'll tell you what happens. Religion has been used in most parts of the world as a way to earn a living. And I believe that when you use these things as a profession, like being a doctor or a lawyer, then the Holy Spirit does not illuminate you as much as when you serve others. Looking

*The Purisimas refers to the altars to the Virgin Mary as well as the ceremony of going from house to house between November 28 and December 7, singing special songs to the Virgin and receiving sweets, fruit, sugar cane, whistles, etc. December 8 is the Feast of the Immaculate Conception, a holy day in many countries.

at it this way, the reality of the Gospel, and the reality of Christ's plan, becomes clearer. I'm telling you, I read the Bible and we had so many prayers, but I didn't understand things the way I did when Ernesto came. That's when we began to discuss the Gospel in the community.

The people said:
Those who paint, they're communists!

Ernesto: We arrived with lots of things because we were coming to a place in the jungle. We brought construction materials, food, tools, medicines and mattresses. Several friends from Managua helped us to gather what we needed to set ourselves up...

The peasants knew I was coming and were here when we arrived. Jose Coronel, his wife Maria, and some friends from Managua also arrived with us but they returned immediately. The three of us, myself and two Colombians, stayed in the church, the only place with a roof.

The next morning, Olivia, Alejandro's mother, came. She was one of the first to welcome us. She told us that her son could come and work here. The first thing that had to be done was to clear the bush and to clean everything. And so the two of them came to work with us, Alejandro, who was about 17, and Oscar, 19. We began to make the adobe bricks.

Olivia: Before long we started to get to know each other. We would get into long conversations with him. I knew he was thinking of working the land so I thought that since we were so poor, I could send my oldest son Alejandro, who was about 17, to work there with Ernesto so that he could earn some money. I spoke with the man in charge, Carlos Alberto, Ernesto's *companero*, and he said yes, that there was work, and to send Alejandro. They paid 15 *cordobas*. That was quite a bit.

We began by saving those 15 *cordobas*. And then we ran

out of rice and had to use the money. But only for Alejandro and for the little one: the one who had worked and the newborn. We still saved some money, thinking about the house we were going to build. We were preparing the ground, and when Alejandro had earned his first 700 *cordobas* we ordered the zinc we needed from Ernesto. Ernesto brought it from Granada. We were getting ready to build a wooden house.

Alejandro: I worked eight hours a day as a laborer. Every day 'til 2 p.m. And then Ernesto taught me classes.

Ernesto: I ordered or bought the textbooks in Managua and started giving him classes. And I said, "You can learn this in a moment." Later a Chilean university student came to stay and he became Alejandro's teacher.

Alejandro: After the Chilean left Pablo Hurtado gave me classes. He taught catechism as well because his Christianity was rather traditional. . . with lots of prayers. He had a manual saying how to pray. Ernesto laughed at this a little bit, without saying anything. I worked this way for a year. I would stay 'til late after the day's work was over. Ernesto would always say: stay for supper. . .

Ernesto: He was not an ordinary laborer. He was quite integrated into our life.

Alejandro: I used to think, now is the time to get Ernesto to send me to a seminary to become a priest. My mother even talked with him. And one day he said to me, "Your mother says that you should go into a seminary. But I think you should stay here while your vocation matures. We lead a Christian life, and you can begin to live the life of a seminary and then you can leave."

Then I really became part of the community. For a year I worked as a laborer and after that I stayed on as a friend and a student. I began to work without being paid because

I belonged to the community.

Ernesto: Alejandro's family needed his wage, but I told them not to worry, that the family would receive a subsidy. In the community work was free, because that's the way of life here: the community gives you everything, and you work for the community.

Our house had not yet been built so we lived in the house we had for guests. We lived like that for quite some time. We used it for ourselves and also for any guests. They would sleep with us, everybody: the poets Santos and Perez de la Rocha, Efrain Medina and the other painters who came. Some stayed a week and some six months. Later, after the attack on San Carlos, the house was taken by the National Guard and destroyed.

Olivia: Alejandro was living with Ernesto as part of the community when he painted this nice little painting. It is a work of art, a painting we would all look at. I was delighted. I said that I wanted to paint. I was already used to embroidering; I would draw flowers out of my own head, without having to look at a magazine. I knew that flowers are pink, violet, purple, and that leaves are generally green. So I thought painting would be easy. But I couldn't find the courage to do it.

Instead I hinted to Marita, "Look, how pretty, Alejandro's painting, why don't you paint?" And then she started to paint. Her little painting was nice too, so she kept painting. Ernesto encouraged them. He was the life of things here. He would even take paintings away to be sold. After Marita, I encouraged Gloria to paint. They were so young. Gloria started, more scared than anything else, but she painted. And then Miriam. And finally, I began to paint myself. In 1974, I started to paint.

Oscar: I am from Leon. When I came to Solentiname, Ernesto had not arrived yet. My uncle lived here. He told my mother I should come here and buy a piece of land.

And when I came to Solentiname I liked it a lot. They are very beautiful islands.

When Ernesto came here, I didn't know anything. Only how to use my machete. Ernesto gave all of us opportunities. The first painting I did turned out rather nicely. I liked it, and the others liked it too. I kept at it and got more experience. He always brought painters here, like Roger Perez de la Rocha. About three very good painters came and gave us painting classes: how to mix colors, technical stuff. The rest we did ourselves, that's the way it should be.

That's how we all learned. Afterwards, we began doing arts and crafts. Everything that we learned was due to Ernesto, who taught it to the whole community. We discovered what was buried inside us.

Natalia: We bought land here that had belonged to my sister and her husband. When they abandoned the land to move elsewhere my mother bought it. My husband and I wanted the property for ourselves because the children were on the way, so my mother said she would sell us this piece of land. There were no houses on it then. Rafael Angel, my first son, was 40 days old when we came here to build our first little house. Now he's 35 years old. We came here to struggle out our life, right, Julio?

About Ernesto, well, there might be people here in Solentiname and elsewhere who don't like him. But there's a group of us who are really grateful to him. Because when he came here, nobody knew a thing. Nobody knew about painting or anything. We lived bringing up our children, working to feed and clothe them. One wage does not suffice to send your child to learn great things. You just live poorly, working all the time. The community was like that.

When Ernesto came, he set up a pottery studio and then a weaving workshop so we could learn to make textiles. He brought some teachers from outside, but it didn't work out. Painting was what worked. We all learned, we all discovered how to paint. He bought the paints. He would sell them to us at the same price he bought them for, to anyone who wanted to paint. He provided everything so we could learn. And people said: those who paint, they are communists. But I'd say, it's none of your business, leave us alone. There were groups that didn't want to paint, but now they wish they had. I painted too, but now I have bad eyesight.

The government didn't worry about Solentiname then. In those times, what they did was take the men to San Carlos, give them *guaro** and a little picture of Somoza. That was the joy of liberals, to have those pictures up. And so the people were fooled.

Olivia: People were poor, but there is intelligence in the countryside. There is intelligence, but it's dormant. That's why I'm telling you that I believe more in God: because God makes miracles where they are needed. God frees people from ignorance and from misery.

When I did my first painting I was afraid even to paint water. I felt like I couldn't do it. But they said to me: mix blue with white paint. That's how you begin. I liked it, was inspired. Other people also liked what I did. Ernesto even took one of my paintings to Managua and it was bought by the French Embassy. After that I put more energy into painting. I was painting and observing things more carefully. I even liked beauty better. You learn to love nature more, the beauty of leaves. All the little things interest you, because you have to paint them. It's something that absorbs you, fascinates you, falling in love with all that beauty. And every day you improve.

And afterwards, poetry. I had never listened to poetry. Far be it from people like us to understand poetry! Sometimes you could understand it because it rhymed. But

---

*Guaro refers to any alcoholic drink in Nicaragua, but in this context it is probably a cheap rum.

then Mayra* arrived, and Ernesto told us that she was going to teach us poetry. At first it didn't make any sense. And then I thought: poetry is something we can do ourselves! At first it seemed that we weren't going to be able to make poetry. I thought it was only for great persons, with training, for professors. And I said, we can't produce this. But when they explained the poetry, you could grasp it. And that happened with everybody in the workshops. They said poetry is in the fields, in everything you live everyday. And then I knew poetry was something we could do ourselves. So we began to write and talk about each other's work. You begin to know how to evaluate it.

I learned to read and write when I was about fourteen. To be frank, I learned when I began to sing to a Madonna we had. My friends and I would sing together. They would sing the first part, me the second. You didn't need to know how to read to sing the second part. It was just the refrain, "As John said, so I have done." But I did begin to learn and those were my first words. I learned more afterwards, when I fell in love and began to write letters. At first a friend of mine wrote them, but since it was better to do it myself I learned to write. That's why I say that my life has been a miracle, and it still is. Just imagine, I would tell the Virgin Mary I was going to sing and that I had to learn to read. And I learned.

Now I paint everyday. I am very ill; I have a nervous tension but I still always make the effort, because I like painting. I like it a lot, and besides it's a way to survive. I go down the road and make up poetry but the thing is, I'm too lazy to write it down. I feel the poem and go on finishing it inside me while I travel. I should take a pencil and begin to write it down.

---

*Mayra Jiminez, a Costa Rican writer who began the poetry workshops which became a national program of the ministry of culture after the victory of the Sandinista Revolution.

We began to really understand what it meant to be Christian

William: We are peasant people. Teresita's parents grew up in the country and Teresita herself was born in the country. My ancestors were like that too; my great grandparents were from a little village in the middle of nowhere in Colombia. My father was a public employee, secretary for the town mayor, a kind of inspector. He was also a choirmaster. He played the organ and sang the mass. My great grandparents, my uncles, cousins — all of them are profoundly religious people. They went to mass, took communion, confession; they followed all the rules. That was the atmosphere in which I grew up.

When it was time for me to go to school they sent me to a nuns' school. It wasn't long before I was expelled for peeing in the courtyard in front of all the girls. It was a school for girls, and I was a boy who arrived there to learn and to play...they expelled me for immorality. So most of my education, or so-called education, went on in public schools, where religion was still very important. It's amazing that in this day and age students in state schools in Colombia are forced to attend church every Sunday as a group. Well, you get over it.

The Spanish influence is still strong in Colombia, so conservative, and such a submissive population, especially in the countryside. The same religious rhetoric was pervasive and people were anesthetized. During Holy Week they would go out with a wooden cross and people stuck bills all over it. That was what religion meant. On the other hand there were people who were conscious of the need to solve this and make the priesthood healthier. The winds of change were blowing. And John XXIII helped to change things.

During my sixth year I had the idea of going to the seminary. It was around 1965. I thought that was the way to work for the faith, for the people. I already realized the

Ernesto Cardenal

preachings of priests with fat bank accounts and big meals were lies and hypocrisy, that the poor people were starving. I was going to be different.

I went into the only seminary that would take me, one which trained adults, "late vocations." There were lawyers, doctors, engineers, politicians, peasants, everything. It was called a secular seminary. I still carried the training of my childhood, which was to hate everything associated with the body. Even at the seminary we were taught that desires and instincts of the body were things of the devil. Love was the work of the devil. Women were works of the devil.

But, of course, they said nothing about gluttony, or about being indifferent to the needs of others. You could stifle your own conscience. There were formulae that did the trick; they taught you to be a tranquil man, with a good conscience, and said that you could earn money, do your business, cheat others, and still go to heaven. Really, that's what they taught us. To abide by the laws of the president, who was a crook, a son of a bitch. They taught us, conditioned us, programmed us, to live and maintain the status quo. And they used religion as one of the main mechanisms for that. They did that with all the children.

I went to the seminary to see if that was the way to fulfil my desire to help others. But a year of it was enough. There were too many contradictions in life in the seminary. I also had the false dilemma which the church still sets up for you, of choosing between love for a woman or love of the church. A tremendous dichotomy which states that either you fulfil yourself as a person, as a human being, in love — which they call human, but is also divine — or you fulfil yourself in other areas. One year was sufficient for me to answer this question. It was during that year I met Ernesto.

Teresita Builes: I lived in the country near a village called Liburina, about four kilometers away. My father had a farm with cattle, and also coffee. There were ten of us. In

Colombia you have five years of primary school and six of secondary school. We studied elementary school in the village, and then we'd spend the holidays on the farm. For high school, all of us went to boarding school; the whole time we were in nuns' school.

I don't know if it was that influence or the influence at home that made us so religious. I have a sister who is a nun — a theologian — and one is with the Paulist Sisters. They do missionary work with children, especially in the eastern plains of Colombia.

At school they made us go to mass and take communion every day. And if we didn't take communion, people noticed. If you didn't take communion every day, you felt guilty. On Sundays we had two masses; the boarding school girls had mass at 6 a.m., mass and communion, and then there was a mass with the community at 10 a.m. We could not have breakfast before communion (that was before the Second Vatican Council). And we had to say the rosary every day. In my parent's house they still say the rosary every day.

At boarding school they kept a very close eye on us. We weren't allowed to have boyfriends. We weren't supposed to receive any visitors or anything, though of course we had boyfriends on the sly. My first boyfriend was quite a big deal. We would write letters and what not. When the nuns found out that I had a boyfriend they brought me before all the girls in the school, and the Mother Superior said that I was breaking the rules and showing a bad example.

My punishment was going a whole month — I laugh when I think of it — without being allowed to talk or play with anybody. Afterwards they made me apologize before the whole school for the bad example I had given. And they sent a telegram to my father asking him to withdraw me from the school because I was a very undisciplined girl. Fortunately my father didn't pay any attention; I don't know why, because he was also very repressive.

At the end of the year they lowered my marks but I still

passed. When I left the school I went to work in a school, and that was when I met William. At the beginning I wasn't in love and so didn't cry when he left. I fell in love with him later, through his letters.

William: The policy at the community was that women could only come for a visit, to spend the day...but this changed quickly. We realized it was a bit absurd.

Life in Solentiname was hard but beautiful — to fell trees with machetes, and have your hands full of calluses. I felt strong and full of life. It was like a paradise. It used to be a lot more wild, there was wild vegetation, with lots of animals, snakes, and so on. We led a very beautiful life.

The hardest thing for me was that Teresita was not there. That caused problems in relating to the other comrades, Carlos Alberto — a Colombian — and Ernesto. Sometimes I was an insufferable apostle and often I was in a terrible mood.

I knew I had to solve that problem. From the beginning I said to Ernesto, "Look, I'm going to get married. I don't want to continue living here all upset, but neither do I want

Olivia Silva

to leave. I want to get married and come here with my wife, and the two of us can live on the little island and stay in touch with the community." That seemed fine to him.

By that time the other comrade had left and only Ernesto and I were left, and Ernesto said, "Well then, go and bring your wife."

Teresita: So William came back and we saw a lot of each other. We fell in love and decided to get married.

William: We stayed at the community while the little house was being built. That was a good decision, it allowed the place to open up.

Ernesto: The original plan was being changed. The brothers knew they didn't want to be monks. And so we couldn't make the community into a monastery. It was a commune. For example, instead of traditional habits, I proposed our clothes be blue jeans and a traditional Nicaraguan peasant shirt, the *cotona*. That shirt had almost been lost; I had to look for patterns to make the shirts. Afterwards *cotonas* became fashionable; we made them fashionable. They were our habits.

Alejandro: At the beginning we would get up at 4 a.m. to pray and on Fridays we read the Psalms. We led a very backward life, we know that now.

Ernesto: There were individual prayers, reflection, meditation. We would have breakfast at 6.30 and then go to work. At 6 p.m. we would have mass, and before going to bed, evensong.

The first reforms we made were in the liturgy. The Latin mass had been abolished by then so we started to have a dialogue with the congregation, making everyone participate. After the mass we had communal meals, talked a lot about social problems, but still had a rather reformist mentality. And also a non-violent position. But our ideas were changing. We started to eliminate the more monastic things. We still recited Psalms, but began to shorten that. In the end we only had one session of reading the Psalms, here on this porch. Some said we should eliminate that too, because it was becoming routine. We had read the whole Bible page by page, and we were beginning to read it again. So in the end we eliminated the reading of the Bible.

Alejandro: And then Brother Laureano* came to join the community. He was an evangelical Christian. He said that there was a commitment to love one's fellow human beings here. Natalia's son Elvis came and we started to change and eliminate some things. First the prayers which were not necessary. We changed the reading of the Bible. And then, you know what happened? We started to read the speeches of Fidel Castro, we read Margaret Randall's book on women in Cuba. Books by many people. We would alternate between reading the Bible, Psalms, and political books.

Ernesto: We had a small prayer that we said after meals. After a time some people suggested that the prayer was a mechanical, routine thing. I thought that what they were saying was valid. So we eliminated it too. Most important were the changes in Sunday mass.

Manuel: Ernesto would celebrate the mass and afterwards he would read the Gospel. Each person would get a book called *God Comes To Man*, which is a very clear translation of the Gospel. We would read it and then comment on it verse by verse. Each person would give their opinion. And we arrived at the conclusion that the system we were living under was bad and had to be changed.

---

*Laureano Mairena, killed in a battle fighting against the counter-revolutionary forces on November 24, 1982 at a place called Cerro de Aguila, near the Honduran border. Posthumously promoted to sub-commandant.

Natalia: Ernesto would ask, "What do you think of what it says here in the Gospel?" And he would listen to everyone's opinion. Some people said what they thought; others didn't say anything. Some didn't agree with Ernesto and would have died before saying anything. One time, someone mentioned Che Guevara. And I said: "Che died, but he didn't die. He remains alive because there are others who followed him."

Oscar: When I began to participate in the dialogues I felt relief, I felt satisfied. Many people only preached the Gospel in Latin and of course, we didn't understand it. We were so happy to have the opportunity to hear Ernesto talk clearly and to participate ourselves.

I was brought up in a sect called the Seventh Day Adventists. My family and my grandmother were of that religion. I would hear the Gospel and would pick up a few things about Christianity and the Word of God. But we never had the opportunity of discussing with the priest or the pastor. They just preached. But Ernesto wanted everyone to discuss the Gospel. He didn't like just speaking or reading. When we participated, each person communicated their ideas, and the Holy Spirit was there in what was being said.

Ernesto tried to get to know the people better. Then he formed a group called "God's family" with the older people. From then on we had more confidence, as though we belonged to the same house. The group was both women and men. We lived as though in a seminary. Ernesto spoke about our vices; that was the kind of thing that he was concerned about. The group had discussions with comrades from Managua and from outside the country.

That experience was very beautiful. The Gospel was spoken there as Jesus Christ had wanted. Christ was a guerrilla fighter, not the sort of person to be kicked around, with the imperialist boot always on top of him. The Gospel was quite clear. It told of the suffering that

Christ underwent for a group that was in a similar situation to ours in Nicaragua under Somoza. Earlier we had thought we could always live like that, with the Book in our hands, without any change. Because many people, even the oldest men, believe that you can be saved by the Bible alone. After hearing the Gospel we saw more clearly what Jesus Christ wanted, what kind of love he had for his people. We saw that you had to overthrow imperialism to live a little better.

I used to think that Somoza had given us something. I didn't feel the need for change, the need to struggle to overthrow the dictatorship. I was quite mistaken. With time, I came to feel hatred against Somoza's rule here. I remember that we were very afraid of the National Guard. Through the Gospel, through dialogue, this fear went away. I also felt a different change. I began to see the possiblity of a change for my people, for the human race, a future for Nicaragua and for all the peoples that have suffered.

Teresita: Everything changed when we began to understand what it really meant to be a Christian. It wasn't so much the prayers and masses and communions, but something else. Love, really. Love for others. At the beginning we had daily masses in Solentiname but afterwards Ernesto said that if we didn't want mass, we shouldn't have it. He said we could ask him whenever we wanted. From then we didn't have masses everyday but only one or two a week, apart from Sunday mass. And we never said the rosary. We would recite the Psalms in the morning, and then read some other book. Prayer was still very important to me.

Alejandro: Father de la Jara, who was active in the Christian base communities in Managua, gave us the idea of taping the commentaries and told us how to do it. Afterwards Fernando, Ernesto's brother, came and wanted to tape us and make a book with the tapes. Because our commentaries concerned theological questions it was important to write them down. After we did the taping, we saw how we were developing politically. Within the context of the Gospel, we were overcoming theoretical problems. The tapes helped us improve our discussions and made us realize how important they were.

Other influences helped. We had a large library, and lots of visitors, although we were more and more selective. And that helped a lot. University students came with their Christian faith and their Marxism, and all their skills. We soon changed from receiving only Christians to receiving others too. We discussed all that, and became more politically aware. In this way we kept growing.

Olivia: You see, before that I would read the Bible with my daughter and would try to be resigned in my misery, waiting for death in order to enjoy happiness. Now I see that is absurd.

Manuel: Those who taught us that religion, and said that we shouldn't hate anybody, had us supporting Somoza's government. In that sense we supported Somoza. Religion taught us that we had to have a dictator there, for God had put him there, that we had to spend our time praying for this man to be healthy. That's what religion taught us, to accept the conditions of life that we had.

Olivia: I believe that still happens, even in Nicaragua, in any place where some people still live in conformity, in their misery, expecting to go to their reward. What will they enjoy then? What we have to enjoy is this life here and now, which God made for all of us. I got to the point where I could not live resigned to eating next-to-nothing, bringing up my children in such poverty, with all my childbirths, everything.

Manuel: They would say: God wants it that way, we have to be on His side. This is a commandment of God. For instance, the evangelists read the verses from the Bible to teach you that each country has to have a government, and that we must help it, protect it, and pray for it. They said that it is a sin to kill a National Guard or to join the guerrillas, and if we agreed with the guerrillas or supported assassins who went around in the mountains killing, we would burn in hell.

At that point, for me, Che Guevara was just a creep. But when Ernesto put some politics in the Gospel, we began to realize much of what we had learned was not true, that Che Guevara was better than a priest, better than a bishop, better than the Pope. That this man went around changing the system so we could live better.

Now, there were some people who accepted what Ernesto told them, but some people did not. They did not believe in Ernesto. For example, some didn't believe in the baptisms that he celebrated. When Ernesto was going to baptize a child he said: "Bring some water from the beach to baptize the child." People said that was not right, because the water had not been blessed. It wasn't holy water. And that would not do. But of course what really works are the words, the commitment that you make at a wedding or a baptism. In Christianity, that's what counts; not the rites, which are meaningless.

Ernesto: Some people complained because we took the statues of saints away. We only left two of them, beautiful antique sculptures. But we burned the others. They were ugly, painted with lead.

Natalia: Some people said they wouldn't go to mass because Ernesto was a communist. They would say, "Everybody who goes there is a communist." Ernesto told the people in Mancarroncito that we would all go there in a boat and he would say mass. They had said they could not come here, and when Ernesto went, there wasn't a soul to be seen. And when we saw that we said, "Ernesto, let's go, what's the point?" We knew they were afraid to come because people said Ernesto was a communist. The rumor was that anybody coming to see Ernesto was going to end up in jail. Even some of the people here believed it too.

And then I would ask them: do you know what a communist is? If Ernesto asks you what it means to be a communist, you won't be able to answer. There are different kinds of communists. To be a communist is to be in a community together. But they would say, what does Natalia know anyway? Ernesto is brainwashing all the old women, after they've already sold their sons to him. They thought he was paying us and that he was turning our sons into communists. That's how they talked.

William: We were in touch with a Spanish priest who worked in the east end of Managua. He was involved in raising the consciousness of the people. It was like catechizing, but it was more than that. It was a method or a way to catechize that had been invented in 'San Miguelito, Panama. Some Maryknoll priests had begun that work. It was taking up a religious practice, but beginning from your own surroundings, your neighbor-

Alejandro Guevara

hood, the people around you, the life you lived with them. And this practice was not for your individual profit or loss, but rather for others. You worked with them and for them. This influenced us to begin to change our own work with people. The community threw itself into this work. And it opened up to more people, and made relations closer.

Teresita and I began to work with this new method. The method focused on taking up religious duties but the new thing was that now people would see this from another angle, a more social angle, less centred on the personal. We worked with small groups of people, with adults, married couples, parents. We held meetings, and it was quite beautiful. It wasn't a show or someone giving a lecture: we would meet in someone's house, a different house each night, to talk amongst ourselves. We began with discussions and slowly the people became more communicative. The people opened up to one another and got to know each other better.

Olivia: We were among the first married couples to have these talks. Then we would all gather together for discussions. I remember that in the first meeting we were asked — and it was the very first question — whether we ever looked at the injustice in the world. And can you believe that when they asked us some people started to say no, that there wasn't any injustice. Here we were, living in injustice without knowing it. But of course, there are always some who are more intelligent by nature. We said yes, and began to discover the injustice in our own lives and injustice in the country. And we saw that injustice, even the injustices of the home, came from high up. It doesn't start down at the bottom, but rather at the top.

Teresita: We would go to the communal readings. We read the lives of all the saints, and realized that many saints were made up, they were pure myths. We read the Bible several times over. We read Fidel's speeches. We read lots of things, modern history, the diary of Nestor Paz,* the diary of Che Guevara.

Olivia: Those sessions were so wonderful. First because we would meet all together. We were all friends from Solentiname. We were with Ernesto, with William, with Teresita, with another *companero* who was there, a very good man called Pablo Hurtado. And we were discovering a new world.

People of my age were practically being born again to a new reality. Despite having been so religious, we were being reborn. Each day we would learn new things, and I tell you that this is the sort of thing where you couldn't take it in and just live in peace. You begin to feel more committed, more concerned about others. If, living the life we led, we were concerned about all our neighbors, now we had concern for everything in the country. And afterwards, for everything not only in the country, but in Central America. And for what was happening in the world. We discovered so many things through the Gospel. My whole liberation. Ernesto had great wisdom, he gave me light. I'm telling you we had been living so drugged in Nicaragua.

About this whole question of communism, and all the things that people took into their heads: I knew it was all absurd. If we were communists or if anything of ours was communist, then it must have been because Christ was the first communist. In any case, if we look at the life of Christ and of the first Christians, his sons, there you can see communism and touch it: they shared everything they had.

Nevertheless, many people were rather ignorant, and they withdrew one by one. I saw some old people who led a really depressing life. They worked even on Sundays, worked as hard as oxen, and they said that they wanted nothing to do with communism. Some worried that the

*Nestor Paz was a Bolivian seminary student who joined the guerrilla movement in his country and eventually starved to death in the mountains. The diary and letters he wrote are a modern classic of Latin American literature.

communists might take away their four chickens, which was all they had. Others said they wanted to "be free" and work only when they wanted to. And that was from some old people who worked all the time, even at night.

William: We wanted communities like ours to be established throughout the country. Our community alone would not harm Somoza at all. We could question his rule, but not harm him.

Then when Ernesto went to Cuba as a judge for the Casa de las Americas poetry contest in 1970, the young people began to say: what about us? You're only working with the old people. We need a club for young people, we want to have ping-pong games, baseball and football. We want to have fun. Our life is boring; there are no amusements, only drinking *guaro*.

Olivia: While all of us married couples discussed the Gospel after the mass the young people would play in the square in front of us, where the park is now. All the young people would play there, up to 18 or 20 years old, including all my daughters. At one meeting I said: why don't we call on the young people too? I thought that we had a good thing — not an alienating religion or anything like that. Why don't we invite the young people so that they can participate with us? So we started a club for the young. You can see the results. They showed a lot of solidarity.

Alejandro: We began to pull together the youth in Solentiname. We wanted to organize all the young people of the region, in San Carlos, in San Miguel, in Santa Cruz. Our first trip was to San Carlos, a very corrupt town with National Guards and prostitutes. But despite that, we organized the young people there; Nubia's brother Manuel was one of the leaders.

Nubia: I was born in San Carlos. I went to primary school there. My life was the same as that of any other child, playing with the children in the town. My father is a shopkeeper, my mother a housewife. There are seven children in our family, four female and three male. After getting my high school diploma I went to the teachers college and spent five years in boarding school. I went through a great change at that point in my life. I found it difficult to get used to that atmosphere and got more and more shy. Once when I came home for the holidays, Maria — Alejandro's older sister — invited me to Solentiname to meet Ernesto. He was denouncing the massacres that were taking place in the north.

That time I stayed two days and liked it a lot. Bosco, Olivia's son-in-law, gave me the idea of staying on as the schoolteacher and we spoke with Ernesto about it that Sunday. I went back to San Carlos for a week and then came back here and stayed as the teacher. Alejandro likes to say that he was the one who promoted my staying here, but it's not true.

Ernesto: We found that our previous schoolteacher was a captain in the National Guard, pretending to be a teacher. He also pretended to be a leftist, saying that he listened to Radio Havana every day! He got friendly with us, and we were quite frank with him. He got a lot of secrets out of us that way. But we uncovered him and denounced him to the newspapers. So he was sent away, and Solentiname was left without a teacher.

Alejandro: We decided to pay for a teacher for the children of the area from the community funds. We didn't want the children to be left abandoned.

Ernesto: And then Nubia came, and we were able to pay her 500 *cordobas* a month from our very meager funds. We were in debt to the bank; we lived in debt. We had sold the cattle, everything. We were broke. But despite that Nubia was assigned a salary.

Natalia Sequeira

Alejandro: She arrived at the school and began to make improvements. It was then that I fell in love with her. But shortly after that I went to Peru for three months or so. By the time I came back she had already started teaching.

Nubia: I stayed here on the island and we started to go out together, *jalar* as we say here in Nicaragua. He went to Peru for two months and I stayed working on the little school. I made some improvements and Donald helped me. He was a hard worker, and like Alejandro, very energetic. He was always doing something. He made some benches for me, and brought me a blackboard.

I had 40 children, and divided them into four groups. I managed to teach them math, spelling, writing and reading and in the six months I was there they learned a lot. I worked hard, but they learned a lot. And the experience was tremendous. I felt very close to the children, and the children to me; you should see how they still remember me now. And the mothers too. The have asked me to return to the little school, but it's impossible now. There are too many other things to do.

Ernesto: I married them. In Costa Rica, when we all got together after the attack on San Carlos. It was in Mayra Jimenez's house. The ceremony had a Marxist commentary on the Gospel, like in Solentiname, on the passage where Jesus Christ talks about marriage.

Olivia: We continued our dialogues. We discussed the Bible in terms of the injustice of the rich and of the Guard and tried to learn more about what was happening throughout the country. Ernesto brought us newpaper clippings of the massacres and crimes being committed by the dictatorship. We started to follow the events happening in the north through *La Prensa*.

We were beginning to understand how far a person must go in their commitment to the people. They didn't put it to me in so many words, but I knew that we had to help. They didn't say anything to me, but I began to consider everything we were reading. And I knew that I was becoming more and more committed each day.

We still depended on Ernesto. I even ended up saying, "Without Ernesto we can't go on living here." Then they said to me, "Yes we can. It's all we've got. Where would we go?" But I said, "If Ernesto goes away from here, I will go too. Before he came we led such a hard and sad life and if he left we'd be back to the same thing."

Some young people will have to die to end the injustices we have here

Ernesto: My contact with Tomas Borge and Carlos Fonseca* was rather sporadic but continued over those years. First, in 1968 I got a letter from a guerrilla fighter who wanted to see me to talk about some things. I attended that meeting and talked at length with Tomas. He raised the question of the hierarchy in the church, reactionary bishops, a church that had to be changed. And he talked a lot about the struggle. I was in agreement with them, but I still thought that as a priest I could not take up arms.

This was when priests were becoming more and more progressive in Nicaragua. Uriel Molina from El Riguero had just come back to the country and we used to talk frequently. We felt that we had the same goals as the Sandinista Front, as the guerrillas, and that Christians and Marxists had to be allies. I continued to be in contact with the FSLN and had several meetings with Carlos Fonseca. I told him I agreed with everything, and supported their armed struggle. But as a priest I felt that I could not kill. I

*Carlos Fonseca and Tomas Borge, along with Silvio Mayorga, founded the FSLN in 1961. Fonseca was the commander-in-chief of the FSLN until November 8, 1976 when he was killed in battle at Zinica. Borge is today the only survivor of the three. He is one of the nine-member Directorate and minister of the interior.

even sent him a biography of Gandhi. He read and returned it, saying that the book had made him admire Gandhi a lot, but had made him more convinced of the need for armed struggle. Because in India, despite Gandhi, they were in terrible poverty, while in China, where there had been an armed revolution, the system had changed.

In 1971 I made a trip to Peru, where there was a progressive government, and afterwards I went to Chile and met with Allende. In Chile I met many Marxist priests. I even met a religious man who belonged to the Chilean revolutionary party, the MIR. He was armed and semi-underground because he could foresee a coup. When we met he said, "On television last night you said that Christians can be Marxists. There are some people who say that Christians, in order to be authentic Christians, have to be Marxists." I was convinced he was right. Later I went to Cuba, where I had a long conversation with Fidel Castro about the problem of Christianity in the revolution and Christianity and Marxism.

By then I had already made public statements in Managua declaring myself a socialist. I did not say I was Marxist; only socialist. Nevertheless, it was a great scandal. After returning from Cuba, I defended the Marxist revolution, although I still did not declare myself a Marxist in Nicaragua, because the whole liberation theology movement had not yet emerged. However, there had been a gathering of theologians in Costa Rica where people had talked about Christianity and Marxism being compatible.

I met with Carlos Fonseca and Tomas Borge again in January, 1975 after the attack on the house of Chema Castillo,* which took place in December. They told me to go to the Russell Tribunal in Rome to denounce all the

---

*On December 27, 1974 an FSLN commando occupied the home of Jose Mario Castillo Quant, an associate of Somoza, who was giving a Christmas party. Hostages were held and the revolutionaries obtained the release of all political prisoners, a million dollars and the publication of a lengthy manifesto. This action proved to be an important turning point in the struggle in Nicaragua.

human rights violations that were taking place in Nicaragua. They told me that the FSLN was receiving very heavy blows, and peasant massacres were increasing in the guerrilla zone. The plan was to exterminate the peasantry in order to stop the guerrillas. So the Guard was killing people indiscriminately, men, women and children. They were burning them alive in their farms, committing the worst atrocities in order to terrify them and force them to leave the area.

It was important to denounce all that. So they sent me to Rome in 1976. And you can say that by that time I was a member of the Sandinista Front, since I was carrying out a mission given to me by the Front. My integration was gradual. By that time my brother Fernando was in contact with the Front, studying it to see what the mentality was in the movement, but getting closer to it all the time. We were both collaborators.

Here in Solentiname, the young people who lived with me and the peasants from the area who were most identified with us were becoming increasingly revolutionary, fully revolutionary. We had been having discussions about Marxism for quite sometime. We read Mao, all the speeches by Fidel that we could find, and had gradually come to support the Sandinista Front. The young men from the community were anxious to leave and go fight in the war. They began training for combat. Then Humberto Ortega* sent me word from Costa Rica saying that there would be an offensive in which Solentiname would take part, an action in the area of San Carlos.

Before that, Carlos Fonseca and Tomas Borge had suggested to me that I might be an executive member of the provisional government; they thought then that the Front would gain power soon. I said I wasn't convinced I should do it but would if they thought it best. I didn't really like the idea. This was an early plan. Afterwards, the

*Humberto Ortega, who was a leading member of the FSLN, is now one of the nine-member National Directorate, minister of defence, chief of staff of the army and head of the national militia.

Insurrectionist tendency* decided to have insurrections in various cities across the country and choose a provisional government.

A number of respected Nicaraguans, who became known as The Twelve *(Los Doce)* formed a group in support of the FSLN in 1977. The first thing they did was write a public letter saying that the political crisis in Nicaragua could only be solved with the full participation of the FSLN. This group included well-known people: some in finance, others who were priests, and intellectuals like Sergio Ramirez. They carried out campaigns abroad in favor of the Sandinista Front. There were some meetings outside the country with all of them. The idea was that they would form part of a new government. My brother was a member. I had not been included, possibly because I had been making too much noise about being a Marxist and they were choosing a group of people who would not rock the boat, not provoke American aggression.

At Solentiname the threat was growing. I knew that at any time the National Guard could come to get me, put me in jail and kill us all. And destroy everything. A few months after the boys began military training on the island, I had started to take the most important books off the island. The ones I couldn't take, I hid. But in the end the Guard destroyed everything.

I wanted to move the community to Costa Rica. But the FSLN sent word that I should try to stay here as long as possible, that the area had political, military and even strategic importance. I remember once it was suggested that Commander Wheelock visit Solentiname but he said he didn't want Solentiname to be seen as being connected to the FSLN. The Front didn't want to compromise our position. We were too useful.

The boys wanted to go to the hills, and I had to hold them back with the argument that the FSLN had told me

*The FSLN split into three tendencies in 1975: Prolonged People's War (GPP), Proletaria, and Insurrectionist (or *Tercerista*). The tendencies united again in 1978. Ernesto and the Solentiname community belonged to the Insurrectionists.

they needed us to live here. But they weren't very convinced. Finally, Humberto told me to find the young men who were able to participate in the armed struggle. And young women too, because the Sandinista Front always sought the participation of women. We didn't have many women to choose from. Most had been brought up as peasant girls and were apathetic and disinterested in politics. But there were a few exceptions. Alejandro's two sisters and his girlfriend were the three women who took part.

I called them all together and explained that they needed

The celebration of the Purisima

to be prepared to fight in Solentiname and San Carlos. They went to Costa Rica to be trained; each went by a different route so that no one would be suspicious. They underwent pretty heavy training. Alejandro went too. When they returned they continued training quite close to here, at the chicken farm, a place some of the young people call "the commune."

Manuel: The most important thing we learned in our dialogues with Ernesto was that the system had to be changed. The only way forward was to take up arms to change the system. You couldn't do it any other way. If we waited for God to take Somoza away, it wouldn't happen. God put us here on earth, to cultivate the land and organize ourselves. But God is not going to come and say, "here, I'm going to make this guy president, and when he's screwing you around, I'll take him away." No. It's people who have to organize themselves and the communities.

Natalia: I began to understand that they wanted to throw Somoza out. I was afraid. I knew that when the Guards found out they'd denounce them. Guard members used to come to mass from San Carlos, just to see if they could catch anyone. I realized they might take them off to jail. I was afraid...someday someone would slip and say something. I used to wake up to any noise in the night.

But I didn't say anything, even to my husband. My son came here on a Sunday about three months before he went away. "Mother," he said, "did you see? Ernesto has read us a letter where it says that in the north they are killing people, even children. A man who came from there gave him that letter. And Ernesto has to publicize that the Guard is committing injustices." And then my son said, with a little smile, "I will be leaving soon to go to the mountains."

And then I said to him, "Son, what are you going to do, all by yourself up in the mountains? People are making

war, but what are you going to do there?'' He said,
''Mother, some young people will have to die, like Christ,
to end the injustices that we have in Nicaragua.'' Those
were his words.

That night I talked to his father about him. I said, ''See
Julio, he is going to leave us, because he's got this
idea...The young people don't like what is happening in
Nicaragua, what Somoza is doing. The day will come when
they make a statement...because they're not going to sit
there praying to God, no way! The people and all the
young people are looking for another way. According to
what Elvis is telling me, that's the way it is.''

Elvis came by on a Sunday. I had prepared lunch early
and served Julio and Elvis. They were sitting down when I
arrived with my plate. When we finished eating Elvis said,
''Father, take this belt.'' Julio said, no, no. But Elvis said,
''I want to give it to you.'' He left it there on the table.
Then he went into the room where Rafael Angel slept.
When I went in to see him he was lying face down on the
bed. ''Dear, did you not sleep well last night?'' I asked
him. ''No,'' he said, ''it's nothing.'' And he got up, went
up to the mirror, and brushed his hair. ''Remember me
when you leave,'' I said. He then got up and went to the
window, looking out, very quiet. I gave him the soap and
he went to my sister's house, and had a bath. He came out
in his underwear with all my nephews and nieces. I always
remember that; he had such long legs! Whenever I go by
the school, I always think that he is going to be there, just
like that day.

Later on my niece came in, and I asked her to go tell
Elvis his soup was ready. ''But granny,'' she said,
''Alejandro and Felipe* came by in a boat, didn't you
hear? They took him away, granny. I'm so angry that they
took him.'' The little ones adored him.

''Well,'' I said, ''he'll be back at night.'' But no. That
was the last time I set eyes on him.

---

*Felipe was another member of the Solentiname community who went to Costa
Rica to be trained.

His sister Milagros came from Leon a few days later. I remember that he had asked me if she and the children were coming. She brought presents for him and everything. Milagros waited a day. She wanted to make some fried plantain for him. We waited and waited. Then a boat came by on Wednesday. Still nothing. By then Ernesto had left; he, Teresita and William had gone to Managua although Ernesto had left word he was coming back.

Ernesto: The Front sent word to me that I was going to have to leave. I was supposed to have left a few days earlier to go on diplomatic missions abroad. I went to Managua to get a visa for the Frankfurt book fair in Germany. I didn't plan on going because of events here, but I used the invitation to get a visa because otherwise I would never have been able to leave the country. The plan was to return to Solentiname and then leave from here. But I got a phone call in Managua from Costa Rica telling me to leave the country immediately.

That was on October 5 or so in 1977. And I sent word to the community that I was not going to return. They were already in a military frame of mind. The place had practically turned into an army camp. That's when I went to Costa Rica.

William: Towards the end, when the takeover of San Carlos was being discussed, our family talked about how we would participate. Not directly, not in the attack. I wasn't going to fight. But we knew that the young men were going into action, and we received orders to leave Solentiname, leave the country and go to San Jose, in Costa Rica.

Myself and another comrade who was there at the time — Mario Avila, a singer and musician — had to take up our position in San Jose. The Front was going to take Rivas, the largest city in the south, and someone had to operate the radio in Costa Rica and start transmitting, calling on the population. It was proposed that I do that work. Three of us received orders to leave: Ernesto, Fernando Cardenal and myself.

But when we left, a shipment of arms for the Front fell to the enemy, near the border at Quezada. They were going to bring in arms through the San Juan river, but they were intercepted. As a result security became very tight, especially for people going to San Jose. So they told us to go to Colombia. We did that, and awaited news of what was happening here.

Olivia: When we arrived back in Solentiname in October from Costa Rica — we had been there since September —

William Agudelo

Alejandro told me I had to go back to Costa Rica for another week. Important events were to take place in Nicaragua. I was not afraid because he explained it as being easy. Attacks were going to happen all through Nicaragua, and then the FSLN would take power. Alejandro knew that if I had stayed in Solentiname we would all have been killed. By then six of my children and Miguel, my nephew, were participating in the attack. Almost my whole family.

I had to accept it. I couldn't disappoint him or say "Don't go." Because I knew that it was a matter of victory or death. Besides, the Gospel tells us that. The Bible says that he who gives up his life will be saved, but he who wants to save it for himself will lose it. Frankly, it had to happen.

Alejandro told me the exact date planned for the takeover of San Carlos. They were going to take over the army headquarters and go underground. We had to leave all our belongings and leave Solentiname for safety. The day before the takeover they came but could only see us to the river crossing and then they went to San Carlos. They were so busy, they couldn't take us right to the border as they had planned. I crossed the river with Laureano's wife, the smaller children, and with Esperanza, who was pregnant. We were going to cross over in two boats, and then they would return on a smaller boat.

Manuel: It was about 10 a.m. the day of the attack when I heard the news that a group of guerrillas had gone to San Carlos,* and that one person had been identified as Juan Bosco Centeno, Alejandro's brother-in-law. I only knew him as Bosco. I told myself it was another Bosco. I was

---

*On October 13, 1977 a small group of combatants from the FSLN Tercerista faction attacked San Carlos barracks. Many were from Solentiname. The attack was a failure and two of the Solentiname men were killed and one imprisoned. The rest escaped to Costa Rica. This action, which was supposed to have been synchronized with others across the country—leading to a full insurrection—did not accomplish what was intended. Nevertheless it was important in the progression of the overall struggle.

very nervous. I went to a neighbor's house, the Ortegas, to find out more news. Adam's mother said, "Manuel, have you heard already?" "Yes," I said, "I've come to find out how things are. There was an attack and a Juan Bosco was there. Could it be the Bosco from here?" "Who *else* would it be?" she said. "You see what they did, how stupid! Even Felipe is in jail now."

Then I didn't know what to do. I went home and told my mother. I said, "This business was done by people from here, people from the church were involved in the attack." "Oh my God," she said, "and now you're going to go."

Natalia: Jose Arana, a member of the Solentiname community, came at dawn on the thirteenth. I was listening to the radio which was on very low but I could hear planes overhead. Airplanes kept flying by the island. I knew something was happening but nobody would say anything to me. Finally someone said I should know the truth and told me. Well, you can imagine, I was crying. It seemed like we were just waiting there for them to be killed. I knew the Guard would be coming soon. Jose tried to comfort me and said he wasn't doing anything so they'd leave him alone. But I knew what the Guard was like. I'm old and I see things better. And they did come. They took Jose and my son Rafael Angel. Rafael's wife was away in Managua doing an errand and he was alone with his sister-in-law and the children.

After they were taken I spent the whole night in the patio, pacing back and forth. My son, a prisoner. I heard later they didn't feed him for three days. I was so afraid for all of them; I knew what the Guard was like. I thought about all of the young people involved, the men, the women. I was desperate. What if they'd been taken, what if they'd been killed? Esperanza Laureano. It was horrible. It made me sick in my head. My daughter tried to make me eat but I only had cold drinks. I couldn't eat. I would get up from bed and just fall down again. I ended up sick for a long time.

Oscar: When they went away to fight, we stayed here. Sometimes it seemed like we were prisoners on this island. At first I was rather angry they didn't let me in on the plans. They left me, deserted me. But in fact they had to do it like that. I had a big family and was married. I had nine children then; now I have twelve, all living. It was because of that, no doubt. Even after they went away, we were in contact with comrades we could trust. We were ready to leave here at any moment and go wherever the comrades were fighting against imperialism in Nicaragua.

But there wasn't an opportunity, unfortunately. Because when the National Guard came, they took me, Natalia's son Rafael and Jose Arana. And they tortured us. At first it seemed they were going to let me go, but they didn't and I was a prisoner for about eleven days. By the time I was released I was sick. I came out with an illness which was like the flu. I had a fever in my head from being in such a stinking place. They gave me a good beating.

I had worked with Ernesto for nine years doing handicrafts and painting. After nine years together they were bound to think that I was involved, no? They wanted

Teresita Builes

me to admit I was going to attack San Carlos and that I knew a lot. But I denied it. I knew a few things, no more. I used to have conversations with my cousin Laureano Mairena in his little house. He would talk about the attack on San Carlos, but he didn't say what day. Unfortunately they didn't let me know. It was all very quick. And it had to be that way, those that took part already had lots of training. I spoke with him afterward and he said it was because of my children. But I'm not sure.

For a suffering people, for the love of Alejandro and the hatred of Somoza

Nubia: We were very happy on the boat. We women, making fun of the Guard. From the beginning women took it seriously and had a great deal of enthusiasm. I remember that none of the women complained. The training we had was always the same as the men.

I went like any other comrade, an equal fighter. I had a 2-22 rifle with telescopic sight, and Bosco, who's a good shot, was green with envy. Before that, when we arrived at La Loma, the Sandinista headquarters, "Marvin" had given me a little .22 rifle that we had brought from home. I had a fight with him about that. I didn't want that little rifle, I wanted something better. Alejandro yelled at me about being undisciplined; I was to take whatever they gave me. But like a good rebel, I didn't feel safe going into the attack with a little .22. And then "Marvin" gave me the 2-22. A rifle similar to the Garand, which shot well. And I fought from start to finish, because I had enough ammunition.

In the end Bosco did take my rifle away. That was only in the end, when the air force was on top of us. Then I exchanged the Garand with Donald who gave me a shotgun. A 12-gauge shotgun, which had a cracked barrel. I gave him mine because of machismo, thinking he could do better than I. I gave him the Garand to shoot at the planes and I was left with the shotgun. In the end I had to throw it away along the road because it was completely useless.

Gloria was in my group too, and Miriam was with Alejandro somewhere else. But to start further back. First it was the boys: Bosco, Alejandro, Laureano. They went to Costa Rica to get military training. Later they came to give us the same training. It took place in what we called "the commune".

Alejandro knew that we were going to have to leave the country later and on our way to the attack he asked me if I was clear about why we were going and why I was participating. He said we were doing it for a suffering people. I also did it for the love of Alejandro and hatred of Somoza.

Ernesto: That insurrection failed because there was not enough co-ordination. There was only an attack on San Carlos and some battles in the north which were not of much consequence. The San Carlos force had to flee, pursued by the air force and by helicopters, with all the power of the Guard after them. Because there wasn't anything more, the provisional government could not be formed. If the provisional government had come into the country, they would have been killed.

In San Carlos the weak link was the commander, Pluparco — Commander Zero. He fled at the start of the battle, leaving the brothers from Solentiname abandoned, without even telling them to retreat. Later he left the FSLN.

Nubia: Commander Zero told us to wait, that he was going to plan the retreat. Then he went across to Alejandro's group but he didn't come back. By then the people from the village were saying, "Go, girls, go, the Guard is coming. The planes are already flying, you have to go." A young woman gave me a cup of black coffee; she was so pale, even paler than we were. She said, "Go, go." But you feel so brave, there with your gun, you don't care if you get killed. I was with Gloria, Elvis and Donald. We knew we had to retreat. And Commander Zero never came back.

When we were leaving, Laureano came to tell us to join the others. There was a courtyard nearby and we were to meet there. On the way we found a comrade, "El Chato", wounded and lying on the ground and carried him with us. I was a bit of a rebel and didn't want to give up. Alejandro said we weren't going to leave. He was going to get the Browning ready to fight the planes.

Ernesto: They had no way out. There had been no plan for retreat because insurrections were to happen everywhere. The order was: fire, and no retreat. And then they realized that the chief had gone away with a group and only the ones from Solentiname were left. Nobody would have died if they had planned a proper retreat.

Nubia: Since I was from San Carlos, I knew a path to the river. So we decided to try for it. We stayed there for a bit discussing how we'd leave; it was more difficult because of the wounded man. It is terrible, to see a comrade like that, and you have to think about how to get out and whether to take him or leave him. You don't know what to do.

I went to say goodbye to my mother. My house is very close to the barracks where we were. My mother was pale and didn't say anything. I told her we were lost and if the Guard found us they would kill us. I said if anything happens, don't mourn me. All she said was, "My child, why did you get involved?" Only that.

I was in the group that looked for a rowboat to take the wounded man out. It was difficult. Finally we decided to take him to the hospital in a pick-up truck. There were five of us, including his sister-in-law. William "the Jackal", who was driving, was very excited. All the nerves and tension was too much and we had an accident.

Since everything had gone so badly I thought that we

should just try to escape and not return to link up with
Alejandro's group. We went through some courtyards and
I got rid of all my gear. I took off my red and black
kerchief, the ammunitions for my old gun and the
shotgun; I threw everything into an outhouse. And we
followed the path that I had told Alejandro about.

We were looking for the river and managed to find
Alejandro with most of the comrades. I was so relieved.
There were about eight of us altogether. Donald and Elvis
had taken the same path but had left it and taken a
different turn. Once we arrived at the river we needed
some kind of boat. We went into a nearby house and the
woman there said, trembling, courageously, that there
were two little rowboats we could take. She said the river
was difficult to cross.

We waited for the small airplane that was overhead to
go away and then got in the boats, four in each. We
crossed the river, rowing with our hands. We just about
flew. The comrades pushed the little boats up on the land.
From there we walked all day in a terrible swamp. There
were all kinds of animals; you feel them going by, here and
there. The water was up to my waist. I didn't have any
boots; I had taken a pair of shoes from the woman, but
lost them. They were ladies' shoes and ended up floating
on the water. Even though it was hard the swamp actually
protected us. When airplanes passed overhead or when we
heard voices, we were hidden by the vegetation. We
walked the whole day, and me barefoot; I couldn't stand it
anymore. By night we were walking on hard terrain. After
that I dragged myself — there were thorns everywhere —
for another two days.

We reached a river at about 2 the next morning,
super-tired from all the walking, and with all the tension. I
was very thirsty, and I jumped into the river, in only my
underwear. All the women took their clothes off like that.
In that kind of situation you don't worry about anything.
Gloria crossed over, then Miriam . . . but of course they did
better than I; they were brought up on the islands. They

swam very well. When I tried to cross I almost drowned. I was so tired and thirsty, I just didn't think I could make it. I called out to Ivan and when he and Alejandro got to me I was just floating without any strength. They had to get me over to the other shore and they returned to get our clothing, our guns, and cross them over.

Then we had to start walking again. The mosquitoes ate us alive that night. When the sun came up we were still very close to one of Somoza's farms. We had hardly made any progress. Just then the helicopters came back. We were eating some green guavas and they were almost on top of our heads. We thought they could see us so we spread out. The three women went with Ivan and Julio Ramon. Alejandro, Pedro Pablo, and William "the Jackal" stayed there.

About 5 p.m. we grouped together again as if by magic. We were all lost by then. Well, I said, if the Guard come they can kill me. There's nothing to do. I didn't even have a gun. When I arrived where Alejandro was — and I was the first to find him, because he has a kind of cough — I called out to him. But he told me to stay there, that we were surrounded. I said, "No way." If I was going to die I wanted to be with him. I was so tired by myself, lost.

I got to where Alejandro was and that was when I asked about "the Jackal" and found out he'd been so desperate that he killed himself. He had been taken prisoner by the Guard before and did not want to fall into their hands again. He always said that if the Guard got us it would be terrible. Alejandro told him to be patient. Pedro Pablo was a bit further over, Alejandro in the middle and William on the other side. They heard a single shot. He killed himself in a moment of desperation. When I saw his body, I wanted to take his shotgun away. Alejandro didn't want me to but I knew we needed it. He was all stiff, I had to pry his fingers open one by one to take it.

That night we were on swampy ground again. Finally we had to look for drier ground. We slept about three hours. There was a terrible swarm of mosquitoes and our faces

got swollen as if we had measles. Our clothes were all torn and we had bites and scratches all over. The next day we found a dry road and decided to take it and risk being seen by the Guard. The air force was still flying overhead. We came to a little ranch. The old man there had only one eye. Alejandro thought there might be guards around but there weren't. We ate and rested a bit for the first time.

Afterwards we had to cross the river again, to get to the Costa Rican border. The old man lent us a rowboat. We still had another night of cold and rain before us, another stretch of mud to go through; but finally we arrived at Los Chiles in Costa Rica. Before reaching Los Chiles we had to go through the cemetery. It was terribly cold. When we arrived in town we looked for the house of a comrade, but couldn't find it. It was impossible because we had to keep to the back ways. We ended up sleeping in a stable.

The next day we continued looking for Maria Kautz's* farm, but couldn't find it and instead ended up on the farm of a pro-Somoza man. We thought he was pro-Somoza then and now we know for sure. The people on that farm denounced us to the Costa Rican Guard. You can imagine what we looked like, our arms scratched, sores everywhere. The people were nervous, but many also took pity on us and gave us milk and bread and things. One young woman in the house was crying and almost threw us out, but in the end she gave us underwear and other clothes. Then when we were calm and resting, they warned us that the Costa Rican Guard was coming. We went to hide in some hills because we didn't know how the Guard would treat us; we were afraid they'd send us back to Nicaragua.

But we couldn't run anymore. They surrounded the place and took us prisoner. They were quite good really. They gave us food and we slept wonderfully. Prisoners, but on comfortable mattresses. The next day after the interviews with the press and all that, they took us to San

*Maria Kautz is the wife of Jose Coronel Urtecho, the well-known Nicaraguan poet.

Jose on a little plane. We also had a smaller plane, armed, as escort. Somoza's air force was still flying over Los Chiles.

Donald and Elvis are missing, but they'll turn up

Manuel: Certain books were left here in Solentiname but only the people who were in agreement with Ernesto had them, not everyone. And then when the Guard came they took some away and burned the others on the spot. The Marxist books, Leninist books, Castroist books — they were set on fire and burned.

But they took *The Gospel in Solentiname** away with them. They went to get it from a Spanish lady who had come here and was going to start a school. She had a little house and books that Ernesto had given her. The Guard went to her house and made her come out in her nightgown. She didn't realize what was happening. They asked her about Father Cardenal and tried to trick her into telling them about the guerrillas — "Father Cardenal's guerrillas", as they called them. Then they asked her about Father Cardenal's library. She said, "It was a good library. There is no library in all of Nicaragua like it." When they asked her about the communist and pro-Castro books she said, "A good library has to have everything, communist books, Marxist books, Bibles, everything. Otherwise it's no good; he's not just going to have comic books and fairy tales. He has to have everything."

Finally she had to show them the books she had. That's when they took *The Gospel in Solentiname*. I was nervous about that. In the book I said some bad things about Somoza. When the Guard got hold of it they'd look and find all our names.

Later the Guard did end up at my place. They

*A collection of Bible readings and a commentary on the experiences of the Solentiname community by Ernesto Cardenal.

surrounded the house and some came inside. A corporal said to me, "Hello man, are you Manuel Alvarado? Tell me, did you go to church?"

"Yes, I'm Manual Alvarado and I went to church."

"And what did you go for?"

"To hear mass," I said. Everyone went, not just me.

"Did you know about the guerrillas who were there?"

"No," I said, "I didn't realize it, I didn't know anything."

"But you went there? And what did the Father say? What did he teach you?"

I told him we commented on the Gospel, that was all.

"And he didn't talk about communism?"

"I never heard him talk about that."

"Aha, and you know all the guerrillas who left?"

Yes, I told him.

"How did you know them?"

"Because they were from here," I said. "I was born here and they were born here. I know them all."

"But you didn't know anything?"

"No," I said, "how was I to know? If I had known I wouldn't still be here; I would have left. Besides, you are wasting your time. The ones who went to the attack are not here. There isn't anything here anymore, it's all finished. None of us know anything."

He asked if I had arms. He wanted to know where I could get them. I said, "If you want, come in the house and search it." At that moment I remembered I had some books Ernesto had lent me under a suitcase of clean laundry. I went in after him. "Look," I said, "there's nothing here. This is my suitcase, a suitcase of my mother's, search it if you want, this is just clean laundry." He didn't stay long and went outside again. He said, "There's nothing here."

Olivia: We left so late we could hear the shooting on the way, without knowing what was happening. We came to a river full of vegetation, a very wide river, and the motorboats there didn't work. We had to keep going. We knew that if the air force spotted us they'd kill us. We spent quite the night pushing the boat across the river. About 4.30 a.m., when we were still 40 kilometers from the border, we heard the shooting in San Carlos. We were very tired, exhausted. The river was dark and we had no lights. The mosquitoes were eating the children alive.

We were all in a little rowboat. And we had boxes with two typewriters, a projector and some other things we wanted to save. I felt badly that Ernesto's typewriter, with which he spoke to the world, was going to be left behind for the Guard.

By the time we reached the shore we were exhausted, and slept there. I felt horrible. When we heard the shooting going on in San Carlos, I wondered if in that instant I was losing a son. We could only wait. Horrible. And I said, "Children, get up, we can't stay here." The shooting was still going on. We didn't know how, we just knew we had to keep walking.

We came to Delicias, the first village in Costa Rica. A little village. And we had to look for a vehicle that would take us to Upala so we could take the big bus to San Jose. The people in Delicias didn't know anything yet, it was all very quiet. But soon enough the news arrived, and everyone was against the attack. We couldn't wait to get out of there. A man asked me if I knew anything. I told him I didn't. Other people said, "Oh, but you are Donald's mother!" I had to say no. Now it hurts me that I had to deny my son. Our goal was to mix with the people there and to get to San Jose. People didn't really want us to be there; even our friends rejected us. They are capitalist people, who work only for the money. Nobody loved the Sandinistas then. The people were suspicious; they knew we were more involved than anyone. It was even more suspicious that I was there with suitcases and children. Nobody helped us.

We heard that in Canas they weren't allowing anyone to pass through unless they had a passport. We had no passports or anything, so we had to hide the best we could. I was thinking about my sons and which one had been killed. It was horrible. But we kept going. We didn't even know how to get to San Jose. But somehow we got there and friendly, good people took us in. We were in different houses. And we started to watch the television.

A fews days later, at midnight on Saturday, a friend called me to say that Alejandro, Ivan, Julio Ramon, Gloria and Miriam had turned up but that Donald and Elvis were missing. They said they'd turn up. I knew that if Donald didn't turn up soon he never would. They had either taken him prisoner or killed him. Alejandro and the others arrived in Costa Rica after their release. They didn't know anything about the two missing ones. By then, I knew that it was more or less hopeless. But Ernesto always said they won't kill them; they must be prisoners. Some guy at *La Prensa* said that Donald was a prisoner in jail. In fact, Donald was dead.

After that we spent the rest of the time in Costa Rica. I worked with the underground. So did Alejandro after he was released. His first combat was in 1978, when they took Rivas with Father Gaspar.*

Natalia: About three months after the attack, my husband and I got word that we should leave for Costa Rica. After Rafael Angel was taken prisoner, the Guard wanted two more. "Take the Sandinistas out to a field and kill them," they said. We left everything behind, just took the clothes on our backs. We walked all day, up to here in mud, until we got to Upala. Without eating. In Upala we were well received. There was a communal house, food, clothing. We didn't lack anything. But, you know, you still remember your own things, left behind. The people were very nice, all the Costa Rican people, and when Ernesto

---

*The attack on Rivas was part of the fall 1978 insurrection attempt. Gaspar Garcia Laviana, a Spanish priest who worked ten years in Nicaragua, then joined the FSLN and was killed in action on December 11, 1978. He led the Rivas attack.

realized that we were there, he sent me some money. I am grateful that he remembered us.

Olivia: We left in October, and in November some time Ernesto came to Costa Rica. He had been in Venezuela. We got together with him the day he arrived.

We used to have regular meetings. Alejandro, Nubia, Gloria, Miriam, and Ivan were in one place; I was lodged by myself with other friends. Laureano and his wife were somewhere else; Julio Ramon too. And William and Moncho and Bayardo were in another house. Laureano was in charge of calling everyone. He would say, on such and such a day we will get together with Ernesto in such and such a place. I didn't know the places, but people would take me. We would talk about all our anxieties. And Ernesto would tell us his, what had happened to him, his sorrows.

By then it was clear that Donald had fallen...although really, we knew it before. But we wouldn't believe it, not completely. We had so much faith. And Ernesto would say, "Perhaps it's a lie, they had no reason to kill him." But I would say, "All the fury of the Guard was directed at these two boys because the Guard was so mad at the Solentiname community. And when only two of them were left the Guard unleashed their fury on them. Killed them." Ernesto still wouldn't believe it, and he would go and look at all the announcements of captures. He also went to the Human Rights Commission in Costa Rica. We did that just in case.

My oldest daughter Maria, who lives in San Carlos, had been told by a friend that the two boys had been captured and taken to San Carlos. Many people saw them. She heard that they killed them right there on the farm. They forced them to dig their own graves and then buried them alive. After the war, when we were back in Nicaragua, we found out that was what had happened. They were buried on the farm belonging to Somoza, in San Carlos. I have the photos and everything. Gloria has a picture with her brother's skull. We dug up the graves on October 6, 1979. On October 13, during the celebration of the second anniversary of the attack on San Carlos, we had the funeral in front of the San Carlos church.

Manuel: After about eight months people started to say that there was another guerrilla group forming here, and that me and Adan Ortega were the organizers. A friend from San Carlos told me he had heard the same rumors. He said I should get out, because if they took me prisoner to San Carlos I wouldn't come back. Already there was an order to capture me as soon as I arrived in San Carlos. There was also a warrant out in San Miguelito.

I didn't know what to do. In the end I went to a brother of mine and told him what was happening. He had a rowboat so I asked him to take me across the lake to German's Point. From there it's only a two-hour walk to Costa Rican territory. So at midnight he took me and another comrade. We arrived in Costa Rica about 5 a.m., in a village, Las Delicias.

Shortly after we arrived the police stopped us. I told them we were from Solentiname, Nicaragua. I said we are fleeing from the Guard and came to Costa Rica because we know that here the Guard supports Nicaraguans. He said, "In Costa Rica we give you support, but only if you don't come to make trouble." I told him we were honest people and had no intention of making trouble. We had come to work while the troubles last in Nicaragua. Then he told us we'd have to go to the Immigration office to get papers so we could go about legally. A pick-up truck came by and he asked the driver to take us to Upala, the communications centre for the police. We arrived there and they did another investigation. "You aren't looking for the guerrillas here?" they asked. I said no, we'd come to work.

But that same day I got in contact with Laureano Mairena, co-ordinator of a guerrilla camp near Upala. First I met with a comrade and told him we had no money, nothing. And then he said, "So you're going to become a guerrilla and join the camp?" That's why I came. He took the message to the camp and right away Laureano came to Upala to get me. I arrived at the camp that same day and stayed there until the insurrection, when we all entered Nicaragua through Rivas. That was my participation.

Alejandro: I've been a member of the Sandinista Front since 1977. I belonged to the chiefs of staff of the Southern Front, the first chiefs of staff that was set up on the Benjamin Zeledon Front. The chief and co-ordinator was Commander Humberto Ortega; then there was Eden Pastora, Commander Valdivia, Oscar Perez Cassar, Silvio Casco, Carlos Brenes, Plutarco, Antenor Ferry and myself. Everyone at the same level. Humberto was a little bit more because he was the co-ordinator. Gaspar Garcia Laviana, the Spanish priest, joined later.

We began to plan the attack on Rivas. We already had a good base of support, people who were on the edges, collaborators, safe houses. The day Gaspar arrived they sent the two of us to make a screw for a 50-calibre machine gun we had managed to get. We had two bazookas and two machine guns. We had them on a farm.

Gaspar and I went to run the first errand in a car belonging to another Spanish priest living in Costa Rica, a lousy car that stopped in the middle of traffic that day. He was the chauffeur as I didn't drive. Another time we took a van full of dynamite, with mortars and all that, to Penas Blancas. Gaspar said we were doing fine, especially because we had so many *pesos* to buy food on the way. That was what he liked, to have beer and eat. He was tireless.

Gaspar's death was sad. The Southern Front gave orders for a war front to be established all along the Costa Rican border. Gaspar was assigned to that front. I was the co-ordinator of my squad. The co-ordinator is the first one to die; he goes in front.

During the fighting, Gaspar said, "I'm staying with

you." And he sent someone else to take over a house. And Gaspar died right there beside me.

The Guard had found out we were in the farm and started firing as soon as they saw us. They were about 40, and we were ten. They surrounded us. Gaspar was one of the first to fall. At the end there were only three of us still facing them while the others retreated down to the river. It was impossible to take the dead men out. They said the whole squad had been annihilated but actually only three died, seven survived.

Ernesto: Gaspar didn't want to be a chaplain for the guerrillas; he wanted to be a guerrilla fighter, nothing more. Once when I arrived to say a mass at the camp he said he wouldn't go because he didn't want people to think of him as a chaplain. He was one of the chiefs of staff. He was a guerrilla fighter. I was to take care of the mass.

Olivia: Gaspar was a very calm, but very dynamic, hard-working man. He worked with Alejandro. I remember the last time he came by my house after being in training outside the country. He said we'd be seeing more of each other soon because he'd be doing a job nearby. That was the last time.

We had read the Christian letter that Gaspar had sent to the people of Nicaragua.* A lot of people in Costa Rica liked him. They also believed that the future of our country was with the church. Because in fact, if the church takes part in the production process, the church also has to take part in the liberation of countries, it is the liberator. We here were proud of the way the church was really progressing.

Ernesto: In August of 1978, when the commandos took over the National Palace and released all the Sandinista prisoners, we were waiting for our boys. But only Felipe arrived. Somoza said that Donald and Elvis didn't exist.

*The letter is reproduced in the introduction.

There were about twenty prisoners who were not handed over. Somoza just said that they were not in the jails. Donald and Elvis were put on the list of released prisoners going to Mexico. That was a list of corpses, nothing more. After the victory we found out how they were killed and where they had been buried. Their graves were dug up, and now they are in the square at San Carlos.

After getting out of the dungeons, where he had been for almost a year, Felipe went to a military camp in Panama. After fifteen days of training he went to the Southern Front. I asked them to stop for a while in San Jose so that he could see the streets, the cars, the city. But it was not possible. They went through the city at night, and took them directly to the Southern Front.

I saw him when I went to the camp to say mass, a mass that was taped for a film. I talked to Gaspar Garcia, the chief of staff, about sending Felipe Pena for a rest because he'd just come out of prison and besides, there was going to be a poetry recital and Felipe was a poet.

Gaspar said Felipe could go to San Jose with me the next day. So we went to San Jose for a few days. He went out

with girls, went to the movies. . . and then came back to the guerrillas. Then they sent him on one of the most difficult actions, at Nueva Guinea, where a group was supposed to penetrate to the centre of Nicaragua. Almost everyone was killed in that attack, Felipe among them.

Manuel: I was in Penas Blancas near the Costa Rican border for about a month. That was where Somoza concentrated the best of his soldiers and equipment because it was an entry point to Rivas where we were going to set up the provisional government. He was defending the place so that he wouldn't get as far as Rivas. He sent the best he had, and there was no rest. Mortar fire day and night. Many comrades died. We entered on June 16, and left on the day of the victory, July 19, 1979. When we found out Somoza had left the country we were very happy because it meant that the war was over. The *companeros* were dancing and crying with joy.

Natalia: I didn't find out Elvis was really dead 'til after the victory. When we arrived in San Carlos they had already apprehended the man who had betrayed them in La Esperanza. He was a Guard. The commander said, "Here is the man who handed over your sons." (Donald was my godson.) He asked us if we wanted to see him. Julio said, "No, if you take him out into the square and give me a gun, then I want to see him." The commander laughed.

The poor kids, it's not clear how they were killed. Some friends of mine saw them when they were taken to San Carlos to be killed. A girl from Papaturro said they were shot in a boat. Two such humble boys. They were so peaceful, Donald and Elvis. I never heard Elvis talking back, even when he was a seven-year-old boy, much less when he was a man.

I now say that the people cannot let the dictators go on ruling for such a long time. We, the people, have some blame. So many young people died, so many things happened. I would never advise any other country to let a dictator stay on and on. Take him out, and change. Don't let him be, because if you do many young people will die and give their lives. The dictator lasted for such a long time here because we allowed his roots to get deeper and deeper. So many young people died because of that dictator.

When Elvis started to go to Ernesto's community, he was 18. One day he came to tell us that he was going to work with Ernesto. "I have work there whenever I want it," he said. I asked him how he was going to cross the river everyday since we didn't have a rowboat. "Ernesto says I should go and stay." After that, he stayed there with Ernesto, and practiced what they all practiced. He remained there until the attack on the army barracks in San Carlos. I knew something was going on but I wouldn't say. I couldn't say anything in public because those were dangerous times. But I understood something, through the same Gospel.

Olivia: In Costa Rica we were in a single house, the whole family and many comrades. We always lived with many comrades and I would cook for them all, assisting the ones who were coming and going at all hours. As soon as the victory happened, Maria, Gloria, and Miriam all went back to Nicaragua. Nubia and Esperanza returned after their husbands called them to go join them. I stayed on with a sister, and came back afterwards by myself.

William: On the day of the victory, we were in Germany. A great joy, but also a desire to be in Nicaragua. About a month later we got a call from Ernesto, and we went home for good.

Manuel: When I went to the camp I didn't see Ernesto any more. After the triumph I went to the ministry of culture to see him. It was a happy reunion. He said, "Now our dreams have come true."

Revolution and religion go together; there is no contradiction

Natalia: Of course now we are free, we can speak. Although there are always some hard things. But at least we are more liberated. Because if those who gave up their lives hadn't done it, we'd all be crushed, without being able to open our mouths.

The fight was not easy. So much blood was shed. And this is why we can't allow them to retake Nicaragua. It has cost us too much blood. We mothers, how we ended up! And all those who fought, how much they suffered in the mountains. If Sandino had not been killed by the first Somoza in 1934 then we would be in a different situation, a nice one. The ideas of Sandino were good for all of Nicaragua. But Carlos Fonseca continued the struggle and that's why I have my slogan, "Sandino in front, and Carlos behind; nobody can crush us."

Ernesto: You should take note that Sandino says somewhere that the Final Judgment is not going to happen after death. It will take place on earth, when there are no more exploiters. And we — without reading that text of Sandino — we discovered, reading the book of Revelations, that it's clear that it doesn't refer to the end of the world. Destruction with a neutron bomb, or something like that. It's the end of the unjust society, and the beginning of the new society.

In *The Gospel in Solentiname* Laureano says, "I am 21; I want this new kingdom to happen soon, I don't just want me to see it, I want it to happen in two years."

Before my religious conversion, my view was different, more conventional. I only had the religious training they give you at school. The mystical training of the contemplative monastery transformed my views. If you ask me what God is, I would simply say that He is someone with whom I communicate, someone that I get along with.

We don't know what He's like. There is a mystic who

says that He can't be called Being, because He is so
different from what we call Being. If we say that we exist,
we have to say that God does not, and vice versa. We can't
use the same word. That is, God is something we can't
imagine. Anything that you can say about God is false; to
speak about His existence is false. It is something beyond
every idea or imagination. But for me it is an experience,
something lived, and a love. It is a union. When I say that
He is someone with whom I feel I communicate, I also feel
in union with Him.

It was God who took me to the Trappist monastery,
where I was sure that my life was going to have as its goal
complete silence. But he took me out to a very different
community: Solentiname. And later, to join an armed
movement in the struggle for liberation. And afterward, to
something that I would never have imagined for myself,
being in charge of a government ministry. And I see all
that as a single path: from the silence of the Trappist
monastery to the post at the ministry of culture, obeying a
will.

But since you asked about God, about becoming a
Marxist, I believe that He is the force behind social change
and revolution. In other words, the force of love. And that
is the Biblical concept of God. In the Bible you have the
promised land, where there will be no social injustice,
where there will be no poverty, where the earth will be
divided equally among all the tribes. And since that didn't
happen, because there began to be repression and
exploitation, kings and lords, rich people and therefore
also dispossessed and poor people, then the prophets
appeared to denounce all that, and announce a kingdom of
justice. A perfect kingdom, in which there would no longer
be any exploiters on earth.

Christ came to tell us that that kingdom begins with
him, and that is what Marx called perfect communism. I
keep evolution in mind when I think of the meaning in the
universe. The stars were formed, and before the stars,
matter began to condense, atoms appeared. It all had a

meaning; this planet has had very special conditions for life. First the life of plants, then that of animals, who have been increasingly perfect until reaching man, and human society, which is becoming more perfect until reaching its optimum state. And this will happen on this planet, in this galaxy, in the infinity of galaxies. And I believe that God is the author of everything. And in a certain sense He is immersed in His work, not removed from it.

Olivia: Revolution and religion go together; they are two equal things, never unequal. That is why I say that revolutionaries can be Christians. There is no contradiction. I have heard some people say that a revolutionary can't be a Christian. In truth, is a revolutionary not a real Christian? If a revolutionary does not mention God perhaps it's because he or she doesn't want to. In fact he or she is more Christian than many who say they are. For me, Christians have to be revolutionaries. And among revolutionaries there will be Christians.

The true revolutionary is, in fact, the true Christian. For me, there are no Christians who are not revolutionaries. If I'm told that this priest is a good Christian but he does not love or understand the revolution, then he is not a Christian. And any person who says they're very religious but they don't like the revolution must not understand Jesus.

That's why the other day I sent a letter to Robelo.* It's easy for them to mention the name of Jesus and to paint it on signs along the roads; first of all because they have money. But no rich person is going to follow what Jesus said, least of all Robelo. Beginning with his farm: the food is terrible, and they treat the workers worse than animals. How do those people dare? That's what I'm against, *that* Christianity. In fact, a revolutionary, even if he says he is not a Christian, is much more Christian than the one who goes around beating his breast but betraying Jesus.

*Alfonso Robelo, then leader of the rightest MDN party, now self-exiled and leading part of the counter-revolutionary movement outside the country.

As for myself, if I'm on my way to mass but some errand has to be run, some people have to be taught how to paint in a workshop — I'd rather go to the workshop. There was a time when you went to pray to Jesus out in the fields, not inside a church. You find Jesus in the city, and that means where there is poverty, where the *companeros* need help.

Teresa: I am still a believer. I believe in a God who manifests himself in one's fellow human beings, who manifests himself in the revolution, in what is good for people. It is not a God like they taught us at school: God is up in heaven and is waiting for us. No. I don't know how to explain myself clearly, but I do believe in a God who can help you, a supernatural force who enlightens you and helps and gives you strength. That's what I tell my children when they ask. But you don't have to pray to Him, adore Him with candles and lots of prayers.

William: We don't influence our children one way or the other. We think that they have to see things, and make their choice. If they want to be believers, we won't stand in the way. We don't want our children's attitudes to be determined in the way ours were. Let them see, appreciate, and choose.

Personally, I don't consider myself a practicing Christian or a believer, although I used to be. I have not stopped believing that we have to build a heaven or paradise. I do believe in humanity, the humanity that Fidel says has started on a new road, in men and women and children and people of good will, that is organized, and which is like a superior being. It has the power to transform the earth and transform what it means to be a human being. Reaching that state of perfection is paradise. I don't think that my God is so different from that of many people who work with the revolution and call themselves believers, who speak of God, of the sacraments, and of mysteries. It's the same thing.

Oscar Mairena

Alejandro: I lost my beliefs gradually. It was a process. Now I don't need them. I come from an alienating Christianity. But I've come to see things as they are, I understand and respect people who believe.

I believed in God, in so many things...and I'm not bothered seeing that many people still believe, even in an alienating way. It doesn't bother me. I don't see the religious experience here as something negative. I remember us getting up at 4 a.m. and reciting the Psalms. I still like the Psalms. Some of them are very strong, just and militant.

Nubia: When I am not in any danger I almost laugh when I hear of God. But when I am in danger I do remember. Not that I'm like a little old lady, always saying my prayers. But for instance, when we got lost that day I was telling you about, that day when William "the Jackal" killed himself, that day I started to pray. I asked God to let me find the other guys; I didn't want to die all alone.

In the end I fell asleep. Nobody appeared, and finally at 5 p.m., when I thought I wasn't going to find anybody, that's when I heard Alejandro. I told that to Ernesto and he said it was a miracle; he believes in miracles. Perhaps.

I had my daughter baptized by Ernesto; it was just like my wedding. She was baptized with tap water in the house where I was living in Costa Rica. The house was full of fighters. That's how Alejandra was baptized. It's not registered in any book, here or in Costa Rica.

Alejandro: Faith is important sometimes. Earlier, we had faith in all sorts of mad things. After the San Carlos attack we realized that there were too few of us. But we had a fighting spirit, faith in the future, faith in the triumph...a tremendous faith. We sometimes were very critical, even with our own brothers; it was the time of divisions and splits. But the faith grew, it was tremendous, and it was that faith that carried us to victory.

At one point there were 250 of us in the whole country.

Or fewer. We thought that with that small group we'd manage to get the people to rise up in three days; perhaps it was possible. You have to have faith in the people, that they will support your actions, because by yourself you can't do much. That is how you trust the struggle, and achieve victory.

Ernesto: A French Marxist theologian I have quoted in my book *In Cuba*, says that the church of the future will be made up only of revolutionaries. I believe there has to be a division in the church. It is the division of classes; the church of the rich and the church of the poor will divide from each other. The only true church of Jesus Christ is the church of the poor. And the other one will perish, because I believe that the revolution is going to triumph throughout the earth.

Since Nicaragua has been an example of the participation of Christians in the revolution, I believe it will also be in Nicaragua where there might be the first example of this division in the church. Because together with the great participation of Christians in the revolution, there is also the other sector, the reactionary sector.

I believe the other sector will antagonize the revolution more and more. But they'll also antagonize the revolutionary Christian people, and the priests and nuns who are part of that process. And this won't be a conflict between the church and the government, or between the Sandinista Front and the church, but rather a conflict within the church itself.

Olivia: That's very clear. What is happening is that they're trying to divide the church. The counter-revolution is trying to take advantage of people's fears to destabilize. But people in Nicaragua today are more Christian than ever. Now Christianity is being truly practiced: the solidarity, the camaraderie, taking care of people in the Sandinista Defence Committees, all those activities. Before there was an alienated church.

The counter-revolution is trying to destabilize the church, but I don't believe that will harm the revolution, because in fact Sandinismo is the true Christianity. The true Sandinistas are Christians, even if they don't spend their time beating their breasts in a church. They are working with other people to end misery, to end disease, to end hunger. And that's what Christ did.

Alejandro: This has been an interesting process, because Christians have acheived such maturity that some of them are commanders of the revolution, and most of them are members of the Front. In general, the Nicaraguan revolution has been made by Christians, many of whom later changed but who still see that phase as a positive one. If the revolution had not been built by this type of people, perhaps we'd have more difficulties.

The tradition of religious festivals has been changing too, for the better. Before, the feast of Santo Domingo was one big drunk. Now, there is no *guaro* allowed. People still drink, but the days before the festival you can't buy liquor in the area. Yet people still celebrate and are just as happy. So the festival is preserved, but it has more human meaning, more culture.

Some people make a big to-do because someone had been a Christian and later became an atheist. In 1970-71, we were always talking about that problem. Taking up armed struggle. Combining Christianity and Marxism. How was this possible? In what form? Later we saw that we didn't have to keep turning these things over. Ernesto talked in the universities quite a bit about there being no contradiction between Christianity and Marxism. Here, the revolution has to absorb the church, we have to get along with it no matter how reactionary.

Ernesto: It won't be a division like the division between Catholics and Protestants. That is, it won't be a break with the Pope and the Pope's authority. Theology is not in question, and neither is our loyalty to Rome's authority.

Here the division will be a political division. As great as the others, but for political reasons.

Now there is a need to unite not only Catholics, and Christians, but those of all faiths. Every day there is more unity. This is not a time for disunity. People already know about the importance of Christians in the revolution. We also have to talk of the participation of Moslems in the revolution; of the integration of revolutionary Christians, revolutionary Moslems, and revolutionary Buddhists... with Marxism.

Fidel always said that Christians could be revolutionaries. That Christianity could be revolutionary. That the early Christians were revolutionaries. He has repeated this, from his earliest speeches to today. He said it to me when we first spoke. He was ahead of all the theologians of liberation who later discovered that it was possible to be Marxist and Christian.

Manuel: I believe that religion and politics go together, because according to the Bible, Christ came during the Roman Empire and was killed because he was against its brute force. He proclaimed himself King, and they thought he was a king who would rule by force. They killed him because he preached: "He who has two shirts, let him give one to the one who doesn't have any. He can keep one." That is true Christianity. It is the capitalists who say that religion and politics don't go together.

What happened was that religion got corrupted. If we had always kept to the religion that Christ taught, we'd be fine. But religion was corrupted after Christ died and the apostles were killed. There was corruption among the bishops and the popes. They left behind them the religious teachings of Christ, and afterward the church slowly disappeared. After many years they started again to reform the church and religion.

Oscar: Since the victory we have seen a lot of changes, and a lot of people are happy. The one who is not happy is the exploiter, the bourgeois who was used to living off the fat of the poor peasant and worker. But now workers and peasants are the ones in charge. We have already seen changes here in the province of Rio San Juan. And it's only beginning!

Manuel: I believe that Solentiname is really going to be rebuilt. Before, there was talk of a lot of projects. Ernesto talked about that, but he didn't do anything because it would have been a waste. But now, with the triumph of the revolution, there are no obstacles. There is no danger we will lose anything. Somoza is not here any more. So if we build a school, Somoza won't come and destroy it.

This whole place was razed to the ground after Ernesto left. The only thing left was the house walls. Everything else was robbed or destroyed. And all the houses, the ranches, were all sacked. In this house there were about half a million books; it was a library house. Everything was destroyed.

Oscar: My dream is already coming true. We have a park; we all built a beautiful children's park, which is named after Elvis. Children from all around now have swings. And parents have a place to take the children. It is wonderful. The government is taking an interest.

Our comrades Alejandro and Ernesto are co-ordinating things to see how we can work. And the people, the community, goes forward. There is talk of a dairy, and if possible a school so that the children won't have to go to San Carlos or Managua...and even adults could go. Many more things, many dreams could come true. Things are done softly, bit by bit, but these dreams have to come true.

Manuel: Whenever we are called we are ready to defend our homeland. Nicaragua's freedom was won at the point of a gun, with blood and fire. We are the majority of Nicaraguans and are not going to allow anyone to take away the freedom we've paid so dearly for. More than 50,000 comrades fell to give us this freedom. As the slogan says, *With a machete in one hand and a gun in the other: we are ready.*

Part II: El Riguero

Father Uriel Molina

*E*l Riguero is one of the hardened neighborhoods in the east end of Managua. As one of the witnesses in this section remarks, it is by no means a coincidence that the Christian base communities flourished in the east end and that later on these same neighborhoods played a heroic role in the final insurrection of 1979.

El Riguero is a poor neighborhood. Its inhabitants are workers. Some are of peasant origin who have come to the capital looking for better opportunities and living conditions. Some are small businessmen. There is even the odd professional. The natural disasters and political strife of the last years has created a social and political stratification rather more complex than other similar places.

The houses in El Riguero are small, generally wooden, though some are made of rough building blocks. The main thoroughfares are paved with asphalt or cobblestones, while the smaller interior streets are dirt roads. Our Lady of Fatima Church was destroyed in the 1972 earthquake, and the simple circular building built on the ruins of the old one is now known as St. Mary of the Angels. It serves as a model for other Christian meeting centres built since the earthquake.

The soul of the parish, and of the neighborhood, is Father **Uriel Molina**, and his will be the first voice we hear. Uriel, a Nicaraguan from the town of Matagalpa, was ordained as a Franciscan after studying in Europe for more than a decade. He was the priest to whom a group of university students went to establish what would later be known as the University Community of El Riguero.

And what about the students? Many of them tell their stories, and the story of their community. First, we hear from the now Brigade Commander **Joaquin Cuadra**, vice-minister of defense and head of the chiefs of staff of the Sandinista People's Army (EPS). Second, **Roberto Gutierrez**, now vice-minister in the ministry of agriculture and agrarian reform. Third, **Salvador Mayorga**, also a vice-minister of agriculture and director of agrarian reform. Fourth, the now Commander **Alvaro Baltodano**, head of the Office of Combat Preparedness and of the military training centres of the EPS. And finally, the commander of the revolution, member of the national leadership of the FSLN and vice-minister of the interior, **Luis Carrion**.

We also hear from non-students who were part of the community. **Antonia Cortez**, who still works in the parish; **Socorro Guerrero Lopez**, known as Coco, member of the neighborhood base community, now a lieutenant in the Sandinista People's Army; and Sister **Maria Hartman**, an American nun of the Congregation of St. Agnes, with more than twenty years of experience in Nicaragua. Today she works in the Nicaraguan Committee to Promote and Defend Human Rights.

The Jesuit **Fernando Cardenal** also shared the life of the community. He is one of the priests playing a leadership role in the Sandinista revolution, with the post of head of propaganda of the national executive of the July 19

Nubia Arcia and her daughter Alejandra

Sandinista Youth Organization. **Angel Barrajon**, a Spaniard living in Nicaragua, was a priest who played a key role in the development of the Christian Youth Movement. He also took part in the university community, and today he is the head of the human resources department of the agricultural ministry.

Jose David Chavarria Rocha, known as David, offers one of the most moving testimonies in the book. A

Manuel Alvarado

member of the El Riguero Christian community, he used to work in an auto parts workshop before becoming totally involved in the struggle. Today he is a member of the Sandinista People's Army.

We will also hear from comrades who, though not belonging to the community itself, have much to say about the movement to which the community belonged: **Tomas Borge**, *commandante* of the revolution, member of the national leadership of the FSLN, and minister of the interior; **Monica Baltodano**, *commandante* and head of the mass organizations of the FSLN; **Martha Isabel Cranshaw**, political co-ordinator for the FSLN in the province of Leon; and **Jose Antonio Sanjines**, captain in the EPS who was a Jesuit and leader of Christian youth groups during those years.

Jose Miguel Torres is a Baptist pastor who represents the ecumenical dimension that has been developing in Nicaragua since the sixties, after the Medellin conference. Today he works very hard at the head of the Ecumenical Axis in Managua.

Now, almost three years after the revolution, the central problem for the inhabitants of El Riguero, as well as for those of Solentiname and of all Nicaragua, is not to achieve victory, but to preserve it. In these new tasks, the church and the community continue to play a role. The university students who were members of the community are among the top leaders of the new process. They now engage daily in struggles they first dreamed of in El Riguero.

Wanting to live one's faith collectively and with the poor

Uriel Molina: A hot afternoon in November, 1971. I am sitting at home and I hear the doorbell ring. A group of young people come in: "el Chino" Lau, who teaches at the University of Central America (UCA), Roberto Gutierrez, Luis Carrion, Joaquin Cuadra, Alvaro Baltodano, Alvaro Guzman, Salvador Mayorga. They treated me familiarly, calling me by my first name. "We've come to show you a statement we've written. We are Christians who want to do something. We want a community, we want to come and live in this neighborhood."

I thought it was the most normal thing in the world. "Sure, come here," I told them, without consulting anyone. And within an hour they were back at the door, ready with their mattresses, sheets and everything. They came in and made themselves right at home, rearranging things. "We want the university community to be a happy one," they said.

Joaquin Cuadra: We looked for a place where we could experiment with a form of communal life. Uriel taught classes at the UCA. We knew him as a professor but had no real contact with him. He didn't know many of us personally.

Jose Miguel Torres: There were thousands of young people rising up all over the country. Here in Managua a group of more advanced youth decided to form the university community of El Riguero under the direction and support of Father Molina. Father Molina was then the most important priest in Nicaragua. His post at the UCA and his preaching in the El Riguero *barrio* were signs of the most consistent, most solid work being done here.

Luis Carrion: We were looking for a different practice than we had in the student movement. At first, the important thing was simply that we were living there, that we had abandoned the privileges we had. But after a period of time the question arose: how are we going to involve ourselves? The only structure that existed was the parish, so we joined that.

Roberto Gutierrez: We went to live in El Riguero. We

chose that neighborhood because it had all the conditions which would allow us to live the way we wanted. First, it was a working-class neighborhood and we very much wanted to be near the working people. Secondly, we found Uriel, who came to play a very important role in our lives. He was a serious theologian and was up-to-date on all the new ideas of liberation theology. We found the right atmosphere and a sounding board in Uriel. Regardless of the age difference, we knew there would be great harmony. We didn't see him as a priest, but as a friend, a person. If he had been a traditional priest, we probably would not have gone to live that experience with him.

Joaquin: The *companeros* who took part in the community had something in common. Almost all of our families were from the same class, the Nicaraguan bourgeoisie. We had all been living at home with our parents and that put limits on our freedom of movement. There were always family commitments to meet, you were always subject to a certain social influence. And also the criticisms. For example, our families didn't like it if we went around on motorcycles or on the bus instead of cars. We started to discuss our way of life. The problem for us was that we had new ideas but still lived in a traditional manner. It didn't make much sense. So during the holidays we finally decided to go and live outside the influence of our families for a time. We'd even earn our own living because we didn't want our experiment to be financed by our parents, by the bourgeoisie. We wanted something more pure.

That's when we met Uriel. We went to speak with him about a new community. We established the basis of the relation, how it would be, what we would bring, this and that.

Roberto: We wanted to be with the people, with the oppressed, in the struggle for justice. We found we couldn't really tackle these questions in the family and university environment in which we lived and got the idea of building a living and working community.

At the same time this meant we also changed our understanding of religion. We saw the need to regard faith not as an individual question but a collective one. We came to see that one's faith could not be authentic except around those who are poor and exploited. At that point we did not think of Nicaraguan society in terms of classes; we thought we were concerned for the poor.

Afterwards, Uriel called it the "university community." But that was just his name for it; perhaps he called it that to justify it to his superiors. We were university students, but that name does not reflect the concept we had. It might perhaps have been more appropriate to call it simply "community" without the "university." We didn't start the community because we were university students.

Uriel: The Second Vatican Council pronouncements affected me very intensely. When I returned to Nicaragua after many years of studying in Europe, I saw that everything was going badly: the dictatorship, every-thing...And I saw the Sandinista Front being born. It was amazing. The Sandinista Front was born at the same time as Vatican II. In 1965, my superiors sent me to the only house we had in Managua, in the El Riguero neighbor-hood. That was before the earthquake, when the old Managua still existed, and El Riguero was quite far from Managua. I ended up there, in a little church, with very poor people.

That was a new experience for me: to see barefoot children, animals, people who would stare at you. I began my life there without any pretensions. I wasn't even the parish priest; I was his second-in-command. But right away I began to transform the pastoral work of the church, forming clubs and baseball teams for the young people, looking for ways for them to have fun. I wanted to give new meaning to the priesthood. The result was they loved me a great deal from the start.

Antonia Cortez: Before Father Uriel arrived, religion was practiced in a very ritualistic way. This was the case throughout Nicaragua: processions, rosaries, spiritual retreats...But at the same time injustices were growing. Only a few priests felt the people's suffering, and perhaps that's why they began to work here, raising the consciousness of the people, opening our eyes to the fact that it was not just a matter of praying but also of knowing our rights.

Uriel: Afterwards they offered me a post at the university teaching theology. I accepted and began to work as a professor, trying to put the Bible in the context of Nicaraguan reality. That approach was tremendously popular. Of course, the church was very closed then; there was no space for young people to criticize the dictatorship. I didn't do it in a very open way, but enough to be able to touch the tremendous feelings they had in their hearts.

I began to see two worlds: the world of the university and the world of the poor. How could I integrate the two? At the university I served the bourgeoisie and here in the neighborhood the poor. Every day I would be sad at giving my best energies to the rich. Every day I would say: I am so false, I'm not giving myself completely to the poor. We priests needed the rich in order to survive, but that made me feel very guilty.

At the beginning the Father who was president of the university sent a car around to drive me to the university. When I became too uncomfortable I started using a used Volkswagon I'd been given in Germany. And afterward it seemed to me that even that was too much, and it occurred to me that I could ride a bicycle — you can imagine, in this heat I would get to the university exhausted! The students used to die laughing when they saw me arrive all sweaty. By that time we weren't using habits any more.

We began the community with a retreat at a farm in Casa Colorada called Las Delicias. Retreats were in fashion then. It was quite cold, and we all sat around on the floor. I would write down everything that the young men said. It was a kind of discovery for me. I was not used to dealing with progressive upper class students; it really was a new world.

In the mornings we read the Gospel, with an explanation from my Biblical point of view. In the evening we'd do an analysis of our reality. Many other young people would come after their classes at the UNAN* and after I finished my classes at the UCA. You can imagine how hard it was: from 10 p.m. till dawn, being with them. I had air conditioning in my room and they would all squeeze in and discuss. Together we discovered how to analyze reality. They tried to understand what was happening in Nicaragua.

Roberto: At the beginning we thought of it as a kind of experiment, during the three months of holidays. But when the holidays ended we stayed on. We liked the way of life, especially being completely detached from the social life of our families.

Joaquin: The first three months we lived in the community were great. The experience gave us peace and satisfied many of the concerns we had. It soon stopped being an experiment and became a permanent way of life. And that had a great social repercussion. When we went into the community, all the friends of our families said, "Just imagine, how awful! They've gone off to a poor slum to live with a priest."

Coco Guerrero Lopez: We, the people in the neighborhood, had been in the Christian base community for some time. We knew the Gospel pretty well. When the students came to introduce themselves it was clear they were a well-to-do group from rich families. They told us they wanted to leave behind some of the life they had led in order to live a bit of our lives. They wanted to integrate

*The National (public) University.

into our neighborhood, our poverty, our need.

Joaquin: We were completely liberated there. You could devote yourself to what you wanted, you could study at any hour. And the discussions. . . Some of the people in the group did not move there permanently. They stayed outside but had close links and came by a lot. They were the ones with more family problems. They would stay for a few days, then return, and in that way they were linked to our activity but it didn't cause an uproar at home.

Coco: The idea was welcomed by most of the community at large. The *companeros* went to the houses, visited the workers. Young students would come, form a club for young people, and meet with them on Saturdays. They joined the work of the community. When you interview Salvador Mayorga perhaps he will tell you that he was one of the *companeros* who sold bread at the bakery. Many others also left everything behind and joined the neighborhood. It was a true integration.

Uriel: The analyses of the structure of the society and the economy were quite interesting. More and more students came to visit and things got so intense — it was becoming a movement. Their girlfriends also came and sometimes we would have endless evenings of singing, guitars, music. I never saw any malice, anything immoral. And I used to say to myself that it was fate that brought them here, these young people who had everything but who chose to live in this house. The community they created was not anything I could have even imagined in my dreams. We treated each other as true brothers.

Also, Maria Hartman and the other sisters were nearby. Maria was very different from the woman she is now. I knew her when she wore long habits and all. She was the Mother Superior in the La Fuente neighborhood. When she came to our centre, she was dressed differently, and was concerned with the poor people.

Maria Hartman: I had no training at all when I came to Nicaragua; I didn't even speak Spanish. Nothing. I came to teach drawing and English to the little ones. The fact that my little students had their own servants really had an impact on me. They would come to school with their maids carrying their bags behind them. It was totally different from what I was used to.

Afterwards I went to Puerto Cabezas, on the Atlantic Coast. That's a whole different world! You had a port there, and the influence of the *gringos*. They were seen as the saviors because it was the *gringos* who brought money into the town. The result was that there was a lot of prostitution and drunkenness.

We nuns had a great big house in Puerto Cabezas, probably the biggest in the place. And although it was used for everything — for a library, for a meeting place and so on — I was bothered by the fact that we lived in such luxury. I used to say, give this house to the people and let's go live in a smaller one. Everyone thought I was crazy when I would say that in our mission meetings. I stayed there for a year, and then I went to another mission in Waspan.

Many Miskito Indians live in Waspan. Oftentimes they were Indians who had returned from the mines just to die, sick with tuberculosis. The situation there made it all the more clear that our work was not enough. We did help, but we didn't do anything to really alleviate that suffering. It was like saying, "God loves you, you are poor but God loves you." What they really needed was for us to find more food or to talk about why people have to live like that. At that point we didn't even question our charity.

Finally I was sent back to Managua. That was when I began to write the Mothers Superior in all the communities, trying to get two sisters from each community to work in the poor neighborhoods. In 1970 we obtained permission. Their support was very important. In 1971, I went to El Riguero with Father Molina and by coincidence that was when the university students came.

Fourth anniversary of Father Garcia Laviana's death. Land titles were given to a number of peasants during the commemoration.

Comrades like Luis Carrion and Joaquin Cuadra had just arrived. They came from privileged backgrounds and wanted to find out more about the reality of their country from the poor people. They lived there with us and took part in the work of the community.

I joined them in their study of the Bible; those discussions opened up a whole new world for me.

Luis: One of the first times I saw Maria Hartman was in El Riguero. I was giving a talk to a group of *barrio* people about capitalist exploitation and imperialism and every time I mentioned American imperialism she would wrinkle her face. But shortly after that she underwent a very rapid change. She didn't have a totally elaborated position, but she certainly was on the side of justice, had total sympathy for the revolution, and soon was devoting herself fully to supporting our work. Afterwards she even became an active collaborator of the Sandinista Front.

Uriel: There were about 40 in all: Luis Carrion, Oswaldo Lacayo, Alvaro Guzman, Salvador Mayorga, William Lau, Joaquin Cuadra, Alonso Porras, Carlos Carrion. And Ernesto's brother, Fernando Cardenal, who had been thrown out of the UCA when he supported the students' protests. My only training was from the point of view of faith, of the Bible. We would analyze the Gospels and also learn from them.

We lived in continual reflection, but this was never separate from our political activities on issues that concerned the community. Right from the beginning there was opposition. I quickly became the enemy of the upper class in Nicaragua because no other priest at that time was engaged in such an experience. The hierarchy also disapproved. They said that our community undermined the family. My superiors were quite worried; it was a strange community — students, their girlfriends, a priest who taught at the university and didn't arrive home 'til 11 p.m. and the Mother Maria Hartman. And slowly, connections were made with popular community organizations.

Salvador Mayorga: When I joined, it wasn't primarily to become politically involved. For me it meant a way of breaking with a life I rejected. In my case I didn't even have a very strong religious motivation. Not that I rejected the faith or anything like that, but it wasn't the main thing. It was that my concern was more personal. I was looking for a way of life and of growth that would be built collectively with others.

Roberto: Perhaps most importantly the community was thriving at the same time as the Sandinista Front emerged as the leadership for the Nicaraguan struggle.

Joaquin: The community was the step we took just before becoming revolutionaries. It offered more possibilities, more freedom to become politicized — and we did, very quickly. So many different people came to Uriel's house. Marxists like Ernesto Cardenal came to talk to him. Our house and the parish of Uriel Molina became a central discussion place. There were discussion groups, with people from the university and other places, even foreigners. They talked about revolution, about socialism, this and that. We caught on to a lot of things and became more political very rapidly.

There were three great options

Alvaro Baltodano: It is important to keep in mind that we were politically involved long before coming to El Riguero in 1971. The community represented another step in our development as revolutionaries. In 1967, while I was a student at the Central American College, a group of us decided to go work in the *barrios*. We went to Acahualinca, which is by the shore of Lake Managua. It is one of the poorest neighborhoods in Managua, where most of the people live in misery. We wanted to go and build houses. Even just to put on tin roofs so that the rain wouldn't get in. We managed to get the supplies and tools that we needed. Our plan was to get people to help us but in reality their participation was minimal. The people preferred us to do things for them.

Comrades from the Revolutionary Student Front* also worked in Acahualinca at the same time. The student movement was growing and was becoming involved in different communities and sectors, but at that time we didn't really have any connection with it. Of course they had a more political aim. We went to "help". We wanted to show that being Christian involved more than just going to church on Sundays or attending religious events.

We also worked in another *barrio*. We gave literacy classes but again there wasn't a great response. We worked there for about a year and a half, three times a week, sometimes on Saturdays or Sundays. Of course at that time one wanted to go to parties, but we went to the *barrio* instead. It was a sacrifice, but it was good for us.

We began to realize that the work was somewhat paternalistic and lost some of our original enthusiasm. It seemed we were working in a vacuum, but for lack of anything better to do we continued it. That's when we first got the idea of forming a Christian group that would live together with more of a connection to the community. We were also getting involved in the student movement at the university, at the UCA.

Joaquin: When I entered the Central American College,† the Jesuit school, I became friends with many of the comrades I later went with to the community. I had long conversations with the progressive priests there and gradually over the next four years I developed more of a

*The Revolutionary Student Front, or *Frente Estudiantil Revolucionario* (FER), was the university mass organization led by the FSLN.

†Pre-university, like high school.

social conscience and got involved in different activities.

We started going to *barrios* on weekends, doing social work, living a little with the people, getting to know their problems, and so on. Of course, this was with a paternalistic mentality that reflected our level of political development. We would help build latrines on weekends and at the same time give talks about health and hygiene.

We also managed to get money to buy wood and build a little health centre in one neighborhood. As these activities spread to other schools, including some nuns' schools for girls, we formed a larger group and then divided ourselves up to go to different neighborhoods. Each group went with one priest.

In the last year of high school some of us — not the whole group — began to work on openly political activities. We weren't completely clear about the situation but our concern was growing. We took part whenever we knew there was going to be a teachers' or student demonstration against Somoza. I remember one of the first demonstrations was when Rockefeller came. It took place in front of the hotel where he was staying. The demonstration was repressed by the National Guard; it was the first time I felt tear gas, that burning in your eyes.

We went to that demonstration in our school uniforms and as a result we were expelled for fifteen days. At that time the principal was very reactionary, a priest called Sacasa. From then on he was always hostile toward us. In my fourth year I was expelled seven times; I barely managed to pass. There were a number of us who were becoming more political. We even started criticising school policies. Our graduating class was the first in the history of Central America that did not wear caps and gowns or get rings. We collected the money to pay for the rings and then donated it for a scholarship fund.

We also started study circles and built up a library of books which we set up in a comrade's home. It was organized in such a way that each of us could sign out books. We'd all read the same books and then discuss them in the study circle. At first we studied liberation theology quite a bit. Also the works of Camilo Torres,* the Medellin documents, all that. Then we went on to study Marxism. The funny thing was that at that same time the criticism we kept hearing from home and at school was that we weren't reading or studying anything.

That small group was absolutely essential for our development. We established values and important bonds of friendship and solidarity that we've continued since then. You learned to have the courage to face a group of friends with your problems and hear them respond, even if they were critical of you. It's a practice that gets you used to confronting yourself.

After graduation we faced our first big decision. We all had similar families and they wanted to send us abroad to study. We spent a lot of time in the group discussing the alternatives. The discussions were often heated. One view was that you'd spend four years abroad, get depoliticized, lose interest and come back a technocrat. Others said, no, that it was important to have the chance to study abroad and it shouldn't be wasted. It was an opportunity to offer more to Nicaragua. It was a decision we each had to make.

Some of us decided to stay, even if we didn't learn anything. We'd develop according to what our country had to give. Most who stayed went to university, either to the UCA or the UNAN. Those of us who stayed continued to meet, and soon the question of our participation in more serious political activities arose. This was still before going to the El Riguero.

After lots of discussion we decided to get involved in the movement to obtain the freedom of two political prisoners who belonged to the Sandinista National Liberation Front, German Pomares and Ricardo Morales. We weren't connected to the Sandinistas then, but we were convinced that these political prisoners were being held unjustly. They had already served their sentences but were being

*Camilo Torres was a Colombian priest who, when frustrated by peaceful means, took up arms with guerrillas and was killed by the Colombian army in 1966.

kept in jail. The movement was nation-wide, involving mainly students, although many working class organizations joined later. That was when the first takeovers of the churches and hunger strikes took place. The campaign led to our becoming involved in a whole series of political activities that were being led, already at that time, by the Sandinista Front. Hundreds and thousands of people were participating. That's when we were first attracted by the FSLN's correct political viewpoint that encouraged the widest possible involvement by different sections of the population.

Salvador: Some of us, who chose to go abroad, did so with the understanding that we would try to maintain some kind of collective life. And we wanted to make a special effort to keep our links with the situation in Nicaragua.

Luis: I spent two years in the United States. I thought that the most effective way of contributing to the struggle was to get the best training and then to use that training for the benefit of Nicaragua. It was a rather romantic, naive

Fourth anniversary of the San Carlos action commemorating the Solentiname martyrs.

patriotism, which was linked to certain religious ideas.

My first year in the U.S. was 1969-70 at the height of the movement against the war in Vietnam. There were demonstrations, protests and meetings against the war, culminating in a great march on Washington with over a half million people. Those events had an influence on me. I was of course in sympathy with the Vietnamese struggle, although I didn't know the background to it. That sympathy turned into admiration as I began to understand the mechanisms and the brutality of imperialism.

When I finished my study year I returned to Nicaragua and rejoined some comrades with the idea of helping the poor in some way, still with a charity mentality. I made contact with comrades who were involved in Christian reflection groups. These small groups, usually twelve to fifteen people, were organized with a more conscious political aim than our earlier study group had been. The comrades still didn't have a truly revolutionary consciousness, or anything close to it. But having stayed in the country they were much more in touch with important events, for example the national teachers' strike of 1969, and the first important struggles to free political prisoners.

At the end of the holidays I returned to the United States. But this time I brought with me new and different concerns. I began to overcome the individualist approach to patriotism, which was, in a word, petit bourgeois, and to realize that patriotism in Nicaragua had no meaning outside the struggle of the Nicaraguan people. At that time Christianity gave me the ideological tools with which to break with the bourgeois ideology which had been inculcated in me by my family and my studies. Because when you read the Bible honestly you see that it's a revolutionary book, "subversive" as they came to call it under Somoza.

Back in the U.S. I still tried to keep in touch with all the events happening in Nicaragua. It was a year full of political activity. There were student strikes, massive takeovers of schools and churches, and several Sandinista political prisoners were rescued from the dictatorship. These events had a great effect on me. I realized I was in a place where I didn't belong; I felt useless. Each day I became more conscious that my place was in my homeland, with my people.

I decided to return to Nicaragua. I had gotten over my naive idea of getting trained and bringing that knowledge back to the country. My homeland needed more immediate action. I still didn't know what form the action would take, but it was clear to me that to find out I had to be in Nicaragua and part of the political struggle. So I returned, entered the university and right away joined the student movement at the UNAN.

I quickly became a student activist, participating in all the protest and political movements of that time. Through the Front I began to have a clearer idea of what the FSLN was about. I also had to confront the issue of armed struggle, though I never really felt a conflict between my Christian convictions and the possiblity of joining the armed struggle. Interestingly, the first study group I joined was made up of university students who belonged to Christian groups, but who were already studying the first principles of Marxism-Leninism. And I began to study with them.

Angel Barrajon: The number of Christian study groups was growing. And as the movement grew we set up structures for co-ordination. I was involved in the central co-ordination and leadership.

All the young people came from Christian homes, from Christian schools, and were motivated by Christianity. The contradiction we faced was that the political and social problems demanded a greater response than Christianity was able to give. Yet we wanted to find answers and in fact it was becoming clear that it would be the young people who would have to find their own answers in Nicaragua. So we turned to Marxism as a method of analysis and to the struggle of FSLN.

Roberto: A number of us were already taking part in the student movement when Luis Carrion returned from the U.S. where he was studying economics. We were beginning to realize that our work was too confined to reforms within the university itself. The Christian movement was only just beginning at that point. It was grouped around certain progressive priests: one group was led by Sanjines, with Luis, Oswaldo, Joaquin, Vanessa Castro, Flor de Maria Monterrey, Alberto Barrios. Another was led by Angel Barrajon and included Octavio Rios, Samuel Lau, William Lau, Francisco Caldera, Rolando Caldera, Rosa Maria Zelaya and me. There was also a group with Fernando Cardenal, who was the advisor to what they called the Days of Christian Life.

Fernando Cardenal: When I returned to Nicaragua after seventeen years of studying abroad they recommended that I work with a university movement called Days of

Only Christ yesterday, Christ today, Christ forever! This phrase is used by reactionaries in opposition to the Revolution's *Sandino yesterday, Sandino today, Sandino forever.*

Christian Life. During the time I worked with the group, which was made up mostly of petit bourgeois students who had some revolutionary consciousness, I became more interested in the political movements organizing in opposition to the dictatorship. I had been anti-Somoza since I was a child but I was beginning to understand that a structural change was needed, changing one person was not enough, the whole unjust structure had to go.

After a few months I decided not to go back and finish my training in Europe but to go to Medellin, Colombia, instead. The Jesuit in charge of that course was giving it in a poor area of the city. That was one of the most important decisions of my life. I had developed a firmer commitment to the people but I still didn't have enough theoretical knowledge or profound contact with the people. I knew that in Medellin I would have day-to-day contact with poor people and so would be able to make a clearer decision about what my life would be like after that.

For nine months in 1969-1970 I lived the same life as the poor people. The *barrio* was called Pio XII; it's in the area of Bermejal, on the outskirts of Medellin. The slum had no electric light, the streets were pure mud and almost everyone was unemployed. There was real hunger and misery everywhere. That living contact was crucial for me. The day I left the neighborhood I made a promise that no matter where I was I would dedicate my life to the liberation of the poor. I knew that I couldn't really do anything for that *barrio* in a new city and country. I could do a lot more for the poor of all Latin America by working in Nicaragua.

My plan was to work at the University of Central America where I thought I could best be involved in the problems of Latin America. However, my stay at the university turned out to be very short; after less than six months the president threw me out. It happened like this. My job was vice-president for students. Three days after I started work, the young people took over the university demanding that the school be made more democratic. The students wanted modern regulations and greater student participation in the university government. In the afternoon, on the day of the strike, they asked all the students to go to the gymnasium so they could explain why they'd taken such action. I also went to listen and see what was happening so I could better fulfil my post.

After his speech the student representative passed me the megaphone and said, "now you will hear from the vice-president for students." It was my first opportunity to carry out my decision to fight for justice. From what I'd heard I agreed with their demands. This wasn't simply an academic problem. The president and his policies were completely at the service of the Somoza dictatorship. The students were revolutionaries beginning their struggle through student protests. When they gave me the megaphone I knew what I said would immediately be passed on to the president, Father Leon Pallais. I knew that I would be in disgrace. And that's exactly what happened. It was the beginning of many confrontations between us that finally resulted in my being asked to leave.

The students won that strike. They maintained a firm stand and for the first time in the history of Nicaraguan universities there was an outdoor mass celebrated after the strike. It was such a significant victory that people from many different political parties attended the mass. The mass was celebrated by Father Uriel Molina, Father Edgard Parrales, and myself.

The mass was also very significant for the Christian movement. These were among the first steps taken by Christians in the Nicaraguan struggle. We were beginning to put into practice in Nicaragua the teachings of Vatican II and of Medellin. Parrales was one of the seven priests known as the "Seven Marxist Brothers" who had signed a declaration condemning the crimes of the Somoza regime. I had joined them when I came into the country in 1968. I came as a disciple, to learn from them what it was to be in a church beginning its transformation, leaving the past behind and confronting new structures, ideas and the challenges faced by our people.

We began to take up more concrete political tasks

Luis: Once the community was established in El Riguero we all worked in different areas. There already was a youth group of sorts and some of us worked with that. A small group of us worked with the base communities. My work was with the base communities. Our mission was to try to raise people's consciousness, that is, to present a new, revolutionary vision of Christianity, for social change. At the same time we realized we too would be educated, that we would learn from the work and contact with people.

Alvaro: I worked with the Christian base communities in the *barrio*. We organized many political discussions. We would read the Bible and talk about the need to liberate people. We'd agree that a Christian was not simply someone who just goes to mass, but rather someone who participates in the community for the good of the whole neighborhood. While this was talked about most of the individuals involved only went to church. Even the groups were isolated from one another. So we got the idea of organizing a leadership in the *barrio* that could co-ordinate the work of the different groups. Creating that structure and co-ordination laid the basis for people with organizing abilities to develop as leaders in the community.

Salvador: I was responsible for organizing and promoting the youth movement that developed in El Riguero. At first though, I worked to provide financial support for the community. Two or three of us did that; some gave classes, some sold bread. I worked in a hardware store owned by friends of my family while I was at university in third year engineering. Later I left that job to become more active in the youth movement.

Jose Miguel: The Protestant communities began to get involved around 1965, although it was much later before Protestant support was widespread. But 1965 was the year when a group of us from our Baptist church first became active. It hurt to hear about the young people dying under torture in the mountains for our people. Members of the FSLN gave their lives every day. We felt deep shame because Protestants remained silent while many other sectors criticized the tortures. Teachers, students, university professors, young priests, the political parties. . .everyone made protests, except the Protestants. Yet we knew that the Gospel says that nobody loves their fellow man better than he who gives his life for his brother.

To understand the lack of support in the Protestant community we must go back to the roots of Protestantism in Nicaragua. Protestantism came with *gringo* expansionism, along with the Liberal current. When Somoza turned the Liberal party into a Somoza party, he got the vote and backing of Protestantism in Nicaragua. The spiritual training our evangelicals received mirrored these reactionary politics. We were all taught that the Bible said we should submit to the authority of the government.

When our small group started to voice concern about the political situation in our country we were practically persecuted within our own church. As a response to our budding social conscience, the church sent for several Cuban pastors, *gusanos** really, to provide religious instruction. These Cubans from Miami were men of around 50 or 60 and stayed for over ten years in Nicaragua. One was in the main church, another in the seminary to train pastors and another in Christian education. Through those three channels they overwhelmed us with a reactionary discourse. It was a theological, ideological and educational offensive. They

*Literally "worms," a name used to designate counter-revolutionary Cuban exiles.

Fernando Cardenal

tried everything to neutralize all our concerns. And in fact they managed to channel a number of Protestant youth into charitable work.

By that time I was studying at the Baptist seminary.

David Chavarria Rocha: My class background is similar to the majority of the Nicaraguan people: I am from the marginalized, poor class. I was born in a Christian home. My mother was quite religious, my father evangelical. As a child they taught me the usual traditional Christian morality. In school I got as far as finishing primary school. I stopped my studies to go to work but a few years later I started taking night classes. I worked in an automobile repair shop and hated it. The work itself, the treatment I received, and the relations with fellow workers were completely cruel and vulgar.

Then I found out about the youth movement in the parish. I remember the first time I went there was during Holy Week and they were having a big procession. I knew some of the comrades and they invited me to come the next Saturday. The first meeting I went to was about the Central

Father Uriel and his mother Berta

American Common Market. It wasn't very exciting because they were discussing all those statistics and that didn't mean much to me.

I wasn't very clear politically then; I didn't know anything about politics. But at every meeting the topics had more depth and became more exciting. We discussed Nicaragua's political, economic and social reality. We also discussed religion and the archaic positions taken by those in the church who did not look kindly on the participation of the church in social movements or for that matter in the awakening of the consciousness of the people.

Things changed when the university comrades came in 1972. We began to take up more concrete tasks: support for strikes against the rise in milk prices and bus fares, and participation in the movement for release of political prisoners. This does not mean that the comrades hadn't been committed before that; we were. But we did become clearer about the need to act. Now we couldn't be content to just participate in a demonstration or boycott price increases. Instead we saw mass actions and political organizing as absolutely essential. We even began getting involved in activities like slashing the tires of vehicles involved in strikes and painting slogans on walls. We developed a more militant and practical approach.

Maria: We attempted to form a community, not only the adults, but also the young people, for they give life to everything. It was a struggle, I tell you. Even when you realized something had to be done, you were still afraid. I didn't only have my own fears; I also felt responsible and afraid for everyone else. What if someone died? Many people backed off when confronted with that possibility. And those of us left had many moments of reflection. It was a very intense time for all of us, the adults, the young people, the women, the men. We were people searching together for what to do.

Sometimes things came up that would force us to act. For instance, I remember one Christmas, when a group of young people that we didn't know took over the church to protest the treatment of political prisoners. They arrived the same night we were holding a meeting. We spent the next several hours deciding what to do and finally agreed that we couldn't abandon the young men. We knew that if we really were Christians we would have to act on the side of justice; we had to show the young men we were with them.

We decided to march through the *barrio* with the slogan *The people united will never be defeated.* It was our first experience and I'll never forget it. Suddenly there were huge lights, reflectors...the *barrio* was all dark (there weren't any street lights), and then all those lights and the Guard's jeeps. At first I didn't even realize it was the Guard. I was at the back, and suddenly there was all this smoke, tear gas, and someone was grabbing my hand and shouting, "You, it's you who are responsible for all this!" Nobody was taken prisoner or anything, but they did manage to scare a lot of people. Again we had to ask ourselves if we were going to go on. But it made us very angry. We weren't hurting anybody. We were only marching through the streets, protesting. We had not destroyed anything; we didn't even have arms.

Then came the threats. The Guard came to the church and threatened the young people. They were almost children, not any older than 15 or 16. The Guard came in their jeeps with their machine guns and all. They were innocent boys, and the church was the only secure place. So why shouldn't they use it? We were angry. The anger we felt was part of the process. It convinced us that we had to do something. And afterwards, when the repression got worse and young people began to disappear or end up in jail, we found money to get them out...the suffering was part of it, and it strengthened our determination to do something.

Luis: The community was a tremendous experience in collective living. It allowed us to fight against many individual weaknesses and better prepare for the

Sandinista militancy we'd later be part of. We organized periodic meetings for internal community criticism and self-criticism. Living collectively allowed us to have a closer watch over each one of us and we tried to deal with our weaknesses thoroughly. Due to our own inexperience and lack of maturity, a comrade would sometimes leave these meetings hurt or resentful; things weren't always put in the best possible way. Uriel suffered a lot in these meetings because he was also criticized. Then a point would come when he would say, "I'm not going to participate any more. I can't, I'm too old." However, he too was becoming more committed.

Uriel: Every year, on my birthday on October 4, St. Francis's Day, I would invite all these bourgeois people to the house. They loved me — I was a fashionable priest — and they came in droves and always loaded me with gifts. The students questioned it all. At the evaluation meetings they'd say I was neither fish nor fowl for I was both with the bourgeoisie and with the poor. How could that be, they asked. I could never accept being cornered so I would say,

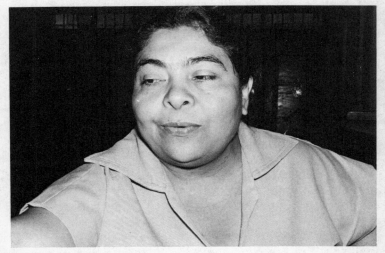

Antonia Cortez

"I belong to everyone, no?" But they'd say, no, I had to make a class choice. I found that difficult to understand.

I also had to deal with the students' families who quickly became aware of the danger their children were in. The first to arrive was Luis Carrion's father. When I tried to give him a brandy he said, "No, Father. Let's not make a mistake. You are my class enemy. You are forcing our children to change so that they'll join a community of the poor and leave behind the culture of their own class." Of course it didn't help that the Carrions were involved in the milk workers' strike. Luis's father was a large landowner. The students would go at night to throw nails and tacks on the road to puncture the tires of the milk trucks. Then they'd grab the driver and distribute the milk to the people. All those things caused a great uproar among the students' relatives in the upper classes. Of all the parents, only two people were on our side: Emilio Baltodano and Roberto Lacayo Fiallos, who even gave me money for a dining hall.

We had open meetings the first Monday of every month. We would meet with lots of upper crust people to discuss different topics, although the analysis usually didn't go beyond Christian reformism. The evenings would always end with a huge dinner. Oftentimes my bourgeois friends would bring big plates of food. Of course there were no poor people there which made it quite a contradiction. The students took quite a hard line about that and continued to question me. They taught me the way. They were discovering how to work and showing me at the same time.

Joaquin: We organized study circles with community groups and with people from the *barrio* who would come every afternoon to the parish. And we would give classes: about the national situation, economics, the national debt, development, etc. That forced *us* to study and be better prepared. Every day there would be five groups coming to receive our orientation. For instance, we would collectively analyze a passage from the Bible, read and discuss it.

Then we attempted to form a neighborhood association, to which everyone belonged. We organized a delegation to go to Somoza's light and power company to ask that electricity be provided to the neighborhood. Another to talk to the authorities about getting the potholes fixed and to ask them to fumigate the buildings. These were social demands that strengthened the organizing in the neighborhood.

Once the people were clear about the general questions, about class struggle and other fundamental issues, they themselves would say: we agree, we have to liberate ourselves from this unjust structure. The bourgeoisie cannot go on holding power. But what shall we do? We were asking ourselves the same questions. We could see that we were raising the consciousness of a lot of people; they were ready for anything, including armed struggle, but what political alternatives did we have to offer?

Roberto Gutierrez

We knew we weren't any kind of political alternative for our country. The only way to effect real change was to be a militant in a political party aimed at taking over power. So we set out to examine the political organizations that did exist in the country. The Liberal Party? The Communist Party? The traditional left? And the Sandinista Front? It is interesting that our link to the Sandinista Front came through a cold, calculated analysis, beginning with strictly defined political and ideological questions. We didn't join because of personal connections, but rather by putting all the cards on the table and trying to examine what we saw.

So we set out to find out about the Front: what they thought and what their strategy was. It is interesting that our decision to find out more about the FSLN coincided with the Sandinistas' interest in us. They had heard that some Christians living in the *barrio* were doing mass organizing. This was tempting to the FSLN. Our class background meant that we'd have access to material resources: houses, cars, farms to use as training centres, etc. And we had dozens of people organized into circles from which cadre might be recruited. We had developed a kind of political structure throughout the neighborhood.

That's when the conflicts with Uriel began. Uriel was always in complete agreement with us, theoretically. But he was under pressure from the superiors in his order to stop our "political" activities that were under the cover of religious and parish work. We were raising questions the church thought better left alone. So it was hard on him. His involvement began to shift from being central to our work to being much less integrally connected.

Uriel: About a year after the community was established in late 1972, I went to Chile, and this served two purposes. One was that I gained experience in a society that was building socialism. The other was that I left the house free so that the people from the Front could meet there. I later found out that the whole top leadership was in my house having discussions with the others.

Meanwhile, I was in Chile and for the first time I saw that Christians weren't being criticized for "meddling in politics." I returned very happy, with two suitcases full of books for the university students. Unfortunately the books were confiscated by customs. I was so upset about those books, they'd cost me $500.

I came back, and found the students changed. They were more determined. Of course, they had made a series of arrangements and were practically Sandinista militants. They never said anything, but they were.

Joaquin: Uriel knew about the FSLN though he pretended he didn't, and we didn't say anything. Uriel was being pressured by the priests so we decided to look for a different home, still in the neighborhood but elsewhere to make it easier for him and so he wouldn't be compromised. It also wasn't good for us that people saw us as Uriel's delegates. We wanted them to see us differently. We had to give our work a different character. We wanted the people to maintain their bond with the church, with Uriel, but also independently with us.

The conclusion that we arrived at, I'll never forget, was that being a militant in the Front was an individual and not a collective choice. The choice had to be individual, even if the collective helped with the decision.

Luis: The FSLN had called. We had the idea of joining the Front as a group, but the Front, or at least the comrades at the time, were looking for individual memberships. They talked about the need to work together. Four of us formed a cell that began to meet and study FSLN documents.

Fernando: The first hunger strikes I participated in were to obtain releases for Sandinista Front prisoners. 'Til that time I had not looked for a direct connection with the Sandinistas. I had been quite influenced by Gandhi and Martin Luther King's ideas about non-violent action and believed that in Nicaragua we could begin a great

Joaquin Cuadra

movement that would support the Front, but through non-violent action.

Joaquin: If you look closely you can see how things developed from the beginning. The first choice was whether or not to study abroad. The second one was to stay at home with our parents or to join the community. And the other key choice: to join the bigger community, through the Sandinista Front.

The struggle of the people in our community

Salvador: It was a very important moment. The feverish activity of the church sit-ins for the release of political prisoners combined with the political impact of the earthquake. In the days and weeks following the earthquake there was a lot of organizing done and it was during those months that the link between the Christian movement and the Sandinista Front was solidly established. The Riguero community played a central role in this.

Prior to the earthquake in 1972 the work we did to free political prisoners took on an increased political orientation. The Christian movement was beginning to have a real presence in the life of the nation. We worked preparing leaflets and organizing groups to distribute them in Leon and Managua. The culmination of that whole campaign was our occupation of the cathedral to demand the release of the imprisoned comrades.

Jose Miguel: Our line at that time was still non-violence. But it was a line supported by the FSLN comrades, because we were achieving concrete results.

We occupied the cathedral the very night of the earthquake. It was all planned perfectly, about fifteen days in advance, with young people from Leon, Carazo and Managua. The occupation was led by Father Fernando Cardenal, Luis Carrion, and myself and involved about 66 young Christians.

Fernando: We first occupied the cathedral in November, with the students from the Central American University. It had a great repercussion throughout the whole country. In two and a half days we managed to get certain concessions from Somoza. Afterwards we had a hunger strike with the mothers of the prisoners, and managed to obtain releases for the majority. Among them were *Commandante* Doris Tijerino and German Pomares.

Then in December all the Christian groups went on a fast in the cathedral. It was a protest against the commercialism of Christmas. We fasted for three days, drinking only water. We were asking for a Christmas of equality throughout Nicaragua, a Christmas without political prisoners. We slept on the cathedral floor — and around midnight on the twenty-third, at 12:35, the earthquake took place.

Uriel: The night of the twenty-third I was alone, taking care of a Cuban priest who had a bad heart condition. He had had a heart attack and couldn't be left alone. I had a strange premonition that night. In the early evening a student from Chontales was wounded in the street, and I went out to take care of him. When I returned I had a call from Salvador Mayorga's mother, and she said some harsh things on the phone, "It's a shame, Father, that you are unleashing the youth against their parents!" Of course it was because the hunger strike had begun and she had heard that it was probably our people.

So with all that I was nervous, waiting for something else to happen. Then, suddenly, I felt the first tremor. It was very hard. Some of the young people were back by then and we all ran out in a panic — not before all the books in the library fell on me, like in an air raid. And the church bells were ringing as though someone was pulling the rope.

The next day all the young people of the El Riguero community gathered to see how they could best help. They had gone to show their families that they were alive, and then they came back. They said, "this is the time to organize the people." Then they went to bring milk and organize the distribution of food. And that's when our great friendship with Pastor Miguel Torres began. It was the first time both Protestants and Catholics worked closely together.

Fernando: The Jesuit house where I lived was completely destroyed. I would spend the days distributing food in the streets and then go to the house to sleep. It occurred to me that this was the time to carry out my dream of joining the students in working with the people and I went to live in that community in Uriel Molina's *barrio*. Before a week had gone by I was living there as one of them.

In order to earn enough to live on we went out every day to sell bread. We had a common fund, and three of us would work every day, taking turns, selling bread in the streets. We lived from that, and we worked with the people. During that time I participated in the founding of the Revolutionary Christian Movement, which was so important later. That's how I became part of that marvelous experience.

Alvaro: After the earthquake we had stronger links with the Front. We made arrangements to read the first documents and a little manual about security. We did that as revolutionary Christians, convinced that Christians in Nicaragua had to participate with the Front because no other party presented a real alternative. There were no possibilities of bringing the people to freedom except through armed struggle. The FSLN was the only organization that presented a just alternative and had demonstrated revolutionary honesty. It had been consistent and always shown honest and revolutionary attitudes.

Why should you start something new if there was already an organization with experience? Besides, even at that time, we admired the fighters in the Front. For us it was inspiring to speak of Carlos Fonseca, to speak about the Ortega brothers, Jose Benito Escobar, *Commandante* Borge. We admired the struggle in the mountains. And as Christians we decided to join the Front and keep working and organizing.

Luis: After the earthquake, the Christian groups and the comrades who were on their own threw themselves into doing humanitarian work in all the *barrios* of Managua. It was a way of helping the homeless, but also of organizing. We formed good links with people and the community became a centre not only for the political activity of the *barrio*, but also for all the youth who were there.

Our FSLN cell meetings were held in a nuns' retreat house in Las Palmeras. We discussed several documents analyzing the national reality and concluded, first, that it was necessary to get better organized ourselves; and secondly, that we had to help organize the whole people. We decided our work should not be confined to the university or the student milieu and instead had to be mainly in working class *barrios*. We came up with the idea of organizing a Christian Movement for Revolution and so began to re-establish links with all those we'd contacted through the December protests.

Salvador: The community was the focus around which the Christian Movement was organized. It was later organically linked to the Sandinista Front.

Alvaro: At the same time that we were building a national Christian movement, our specific experience in El Riguero was being transmitted into a new working alternative in lots of different communities. Some younger comrades joined us and then went to live in another community. Soon things were happening in all the East End *barrios* of

Managua and most had active Christian base communities. This work also had an influence on other priests. It
wasn't just the lay people who were becoming political, it
was the priests too.

Roberto: The Christian Movement had several co-ordin-
ators who worked as a group organizing the work in
different communities. To a large degree that committee
was led by Luis and myself. Our priority was organizing in
the *barrios*. From there we recruited people to the
movement, people that we knew and who were involved in
groups. There were eight *barrios*: San Judas, Ducali,
Larreynaga, La Fuenta, Catorce de Septiembre, Riguero,
Nicarao, I don't remember the other. The work was
different depending on the possibilities in each neighborhood.

We carried out a kind of investigation into the main
problems of each *barrio*: water, electricity, transportation,
health...and then started mobilizing people around these
problems. We worked to reframe the religious ideas of
each community, usually through the priest or other
well-respected members. We promoted a more political
reading of the Bible and connected that to discussions
about the problems in the community. The idea was to
have the Christian base communities become community
organizations which would begin to deal with the *barrio's*
problems and would thus constitute a kind of leadership
for the *barrio*. And that's exactly what happened in most
cases.

That work in the *barrio* had a tremendous impact on the
people and the political struggle in Nicaragua. It was not
well known because most of the work had to be
clandestine, even when the comrades didn't belong to the
Front. The repressive conditions in Nicaragua forced us to
work secretly, underground. We recruited many of those
involved in the base communities to the Front and others
became collaborators by lending their houses, etc. This
experience was particularly important because at the

Angel Barrajon

beginning the Christian movement had been a petit bourgeois movement. This was changing as a result of the work in the *barrios*, which was more and more under the leadership of the FSLN.

We also started organizing Christian groups in high schools. We were pretty selective. We recruited some people and organized them as leadership in the schools. We managed to mobilize the schools around their problems.

The movement spread to Leon at the time of the earthquake. People from the movement went to Leon to work or sometimes to see girlfriends. The two people who took most responsibility for organizing the movement there were Monica Baltodano and Oscar Perez Casar. It was a similar experience, work with the student movement and in the *barrios*.

Monica Baltodano: The earthquake sharpened the contradictions between Somoza's system and the Nicaraguan working people. I was recruited to the FSLN in January, 1973, right after the earthquake. By then I was already involved in the Christian movement. My first contact with the movement was through Ricardo Morales. Ricardo was the one who thought that it was important for the FSLN to relate to the Christian movement. He could see that it needed a little push, that it needed to be linked to the Front in an organized way. In fact we were already working as revolutionaries. The Riguero community existed already and consciousness-raising work was going on in many different neighborhoods.

After the earthquake there was more communication between us and the FSLN and we were then recruited as a group. When we joined we thought our work would change, but it didn't. The FSLN told us to keep being leaders in the Christian movement, to go to masses, everything. They were interested in linking the work that we were already doing with the FSLN. They had certain needs: safe houses, means of transportation, places to hide arms. And people. Our new tasks were to recruit people and to get houses. We were also involved in consciousness-raising. We talked to people about the situation in Nicaragua saying that we were not predestined to live this way, that it wasn't God who wanted it. We pushed people to look for solutions to the problems. This political orientation helped people in their work in the popular movements and those who were more conscious and had more energy were recruited into the Sandinista Front.

It was a great transition period. In fact, the whole Christian movement was being oriented in one way or another by the Front. There were many, many of us who belonged to the Front. The FSLN was very conscious that without a strong and broad-based movement it would be impossible to carry out armed struggle and achieve victory. They knew the Christian movement could facilitate this. The Sandinista Front couldn't work openly; it was an underground organization. But the Christian movement had a broader base of operations. We were less subject to repression. We could go into a *barrio*, talk politics and still be protected by the mantle of Christianity. That's one reason the movement was so important in the history of the revolution here.

Recognizing the necessity of incorporating religion and the religious community into the revolutionary struggle was a great insight of the Sandinista Front. The Front saw that the great majority of Nicaraguans were Christians and so weren't concerned with converting them to Marxism. What was crucial was not that people were Marxist, but that they were ready to fight against the dictatorship. For example, when we joined the Front we never felt any rejection of our religion. The comrades told us there was no conflict between being a Christian and a FSLN militant. If there had been it would have been a lot more difficult to link the Christian movement to the Front. In my case, I continued to be a believer for a long time. It was very much a personal choice to leave religious ideas behind. Very individual. The Front never directed us to fight those ideas.

Luis: The communities played three important roles. They were recruiting grounds and places for propaganda. They were very important in that they served to break the myth about a conflict between Christianity and Sandinistas. The communities also spread a version of Christianity that favored the interests of the people.

The ideological and political activity of progressive priests and young Christians was coming together. Christians were becoming more open to working with the FSLN and the struggle of the people in general was being reflected inside the community organizations of the Catholic church. I'm not only referring to the Managua experience which, though it is the best known, was not unique. For instance, in Chinandega there wasn't an organized Christian movement, but there was great support. Even two Italian priests who had an asylum for orphan children provided a safe house and a meeting place for the Front. Their vehicles were used to transport clandestine people. There was another priest, the principal of a school, who literally placed the school at the service of the Sandinistas. And Gaspar Garcia Laviana took on an important public role in promoting the connection between revolutionary awareness and religion. Large numbers of people were recruited through this whole process.

Jose Miguel: By 1971 the growth in popular movements throughout Latin America was also spreading through the church. Fidel Castro had already made a statement about revolutionary Christians. Ernesto Cardenal, who was working in Solentiname, had visited Cuba in 1970, and wrote his book in which he made statements about revolution. I remember Miguel Obando, Archbishop of Managua, commented on Ernesto's trip to Cuba by saying, "There is communist penetration inside the Nicaraguan Catholic church."

In 1971, while in Chile at a gathering of Christians for Socialism I found out that a brigade of young Christians was being organized to go to Cuba. I was interested in getting to know the Cuban Revolution by seeing it up close, and so we decided to go. Here in Nicaragua we were fighting for a new society, but it still was an ideal and imaginary thing. We didn't know for sure if the society for which we fought could really exist. We needed to see in practice what a revolution was.

I was in Cuba about three weeks and met with Commander Humberto Ortega who was there as well. We spoke at length about the situation in Nicaragua. I told him about the awakening of Christians, churches, communities, young people and schools. I told him about the church sit-ins in favor of freedom for political prisoners from the Sandinista Front. I also asked him to explain to me about historical dialectical materialism. We talked practically a whole day. He explained the basics of Marxism to me. We were together for May Day, which was an extremely important experience for me. And when I returned to Nicaragua, I immediately shared all that I had learned with the different groups here.

Fernando: We had meetings, retreats, or day-long sessions; we would go for two or three days to a house and have talks and discussions about the political situation. Through a Christian motivation, young people from the upper class or the petit bourgeoisie would change their bourgeois attitudes and values to wanting to transform the country so that justice would prevail. The step was from a bourgeois outlook to a position of fighting for justice.

During those days of meeting together, they would begin to see that Christianity is primarily love. And in our country love has to be a struggle for justice. You can't have love without justice. Love has to lead to commitment, or else it's a false love, as St. John says in his first epistle.

Maria: The course opened my eyes. I saw the Bible for the first time from the point of view of the situation we lived in. We studied the book of Exodus, where God says, "I have seen the suffering of my people, and I am going to save them, free them." And then we thought about the suffering of the people right around us, in the *barrio*. We would have conversations with the people, and when you listened to them, it was quite a testimony...what they lived, their problems and their faith that something could be done.

When the Front got in contact with me I felt very happy because I wanted to do more. I had been in the U.S. for about a year with hepatitis, doing solidarity work. When I was in Wisconsin I went and told the aid agencies that Nicaragua was not receiving the post-earthquake aid they were sending. That is, I knew it did arrive, but not to the people. I found out that Somoza had a friend in Wisconsin who was a doctor, and he was in charge of covering up everything. I worried that if he knew that I was making such a racket, perhaps Somoza would not let me back into the country. But no.

As soon as I returned, one of the members of the Front got in touch with me and asked me if I could get some medicines for the guys who were in jail. And that's how it began. I started with a small commitment, which then grew and grew. Afterwards I worked as a driver for some of the men who were underground; I transported arms and things like that. I formed study groups and found places for comrades to stay. Those young men, who came from such wealthy families, were ready to live like poor people. They were risking their lives every day knowing that they probably wouldn't live to see the victory of the revolution. They took a risk every time they left the house. And in spite of that they did it with such happiness. It was quite an example.

Joaquin: We became active in the FSLN and worked together with Uriel from the same base. Oftentimes the people that we recruited into a Sandinista cell or as collaborators were from the base communities and linked to the parish.

Maria: All the university students were well accepted by the people, they were loved. And before the insurrection, when the boys began to disappear, the people would ask: "Where is Joaquin? What's Luis doing these days?"

There are instances, so many cases, of people who took a risk just going to a meeting: family men who put their jobs on the line; women who might attend meetings without their husband's permission; young people who would go out at 1 or 2 a.m. to put up posters. Mothers who were aware of their son's or daughter's commitment who wouldn't say anything; they supported their young people... all these are unknown heroes of the war.

I remember a woman who had two sons. One lost his job simply because he had participated in neighborhood activities; the other one never really had a job, because of his responsibilities in the FSLN. Both were assassinated within weeks of each other. I didn't see her until one week after the victory. She said, "I had to give them up so that we could gain our freedom. But it was worth it."

Joaquin: When we joined the Front, they organized all of us into one cell for a couple of months, but then separated us. Soon only two of us were left to take care of all the work in the community and in the *barrio*. And then I was transferred to organizing clandestine support structures: drivers, messages, contacts. I even had to leave all my university activities and go back to live with my parents. I was not supposed to go to the *barrio* so much or to our house in the community, but lead my normal life in my parents' house, hiding behind the social circles that I come from.

By then Uriel was off on the sidelines. He gave enthusiastic support as a collaborator, and was happy that the people in whom he had awakened a consciousness were

Jose Miguel Torres

now taking steps and making political choices with the Sandinistas. But our working link became much less.

Luis: Uriel was very nervous, very tense, when he saw that our small community was falling apart, especially since we had moved to another house in the same neighborhood. Prior to joining the Sandinista Front we did most of our activity through the parish structure. But after the earthquake, when the Christian movement really began to get organized, we practically left the parish structures and dedicated ourselves to the organization and development of the Christian movement.

Joaquin: People said the community was falling apart, but that wasn't quite true. We didn't really stop being a community. We discussed how the community was now larger, no longer the small group that had existed 'til then. Our concept of community had to change even though the bonds between us were still there. It had to be a broader thing. Our community was now the whole struggle.

Fernando: Through those experiences, through authentic Christian faith, we encouraged young people to take up fighting for justice and committing themselves to the people. Most ended up joining the FSLN because in Nicaragua that was the only authentic way of making that commitment real and true. Some left behind their explicit Christian faith but did not abandon the profound values that had motivated them. Others continued in their beliefs, maintaining their commitment to the revolution, to their faith and to the Front.

The testimony becomes reality

Jose Miguel: When I returned from Cuba in 1973 I began to meet with groups of young people in El Riguero, Leon and Corinto to tell them what I had seen in Cuba, what their revolution had done in terms of health, education, agriculture. What such a change meant. I also told them I had been in many churches, including Lutheran, Methodist, Presbyterian, Episcopal, Baptist churches ...and I was able to tell them that the imperialist propaganda was not true. I had seen a reality that did not include beggar children. That was powerful in itself.

Ricardo Morales Aviles was friends with my sister. He sometimes spent a whole day in my house when he came to Managua. And we'd talk from breakfast to supper. He asked me what I thought about the Christians for Socialism movement in Chile, what I thought about the affirmation of class struggle in their documents...and other things. Very profound things, having to do with the Christian vision of history. We would talk about all those things. I invited him to a meeting we were planning, with more than 50 young people from other parts of Central America, 50 from Nicaragua, plus ten from South America.

We invited Ricardo to give us an anyalysis of the Nicaraguan revolution. He spent three and a half hours

Luis Carrion

speaking to us. His analysis had such an impact on us...and in the middle of this talk Ricardo burst into tears. For him, those political statements were not just intellectual analyses, but truths which had grown out of the experiences of lives, of years of struggle. For us it was a marvelous experience; him sitting beneath a big crucifix, with all those old trees around, in Tepayac.

The next day, Ricardo was killed in combat, together with three other comrades. All the people who had gathered with us were shaken by his death; almost his last words to us were about the need for struggle in Nicaragua. There was even a moment when he said, The point is not who is going to make the revolution, or what label or title it has. The point is to get rid of unhappiness, poverty and barefoot children.''

Antonia: My husband died at the beginning of 1974. A natural death. My children and I were going to leave and join my family but Father Uriel said to us, "I need you all, and you need me. We have been like a family, working in the parish.'' He suggested that we stay living in the community, working with him, helping out in the office and in the kitchen.

Uriel: I used to go and celebrate masses, in the various *barrios*. I did it to raise the morale of the people. And one day, when I was finishing — I was in the Soborio *barrio* — a little boy came in with a piece of paper that said, "I am nearby, in a house. I'll wait for you tonight. Don't fail me. Tomas Borge.'' When I read the note I got nervous, because people were all around. I came very quickly back to the house and said to Antonia, who was with me, "I have to go. Anything can happen, but I have to go.''

A young man brought me into the humble house where Tomas was. The room was very small, very low, and Tomas was sitting with one machine gun on either side of him. There was a candle on the table lighting up a book by Marx, *Capital*. It was very dangerous. He knew that if a police patrol came by he would die. But at 11 p.m. there wasn't anyone in the street.

Borge had been a childhood friend of mine in Matagalpa but I lost contact with him when I went to Europe. He was into sports, was very healthy, and at one point he even wanted to become a priest. When he saw me he got up and gave me a big strong bear hug. And he said, "I'm so happy to see you. You know something? In my long nights in the underground, I live in hope of being able to listen to your words as a minister of God. I've wanted to talk to you for a long time. It's time for us to act together, Christians and Sandinistas, like brothers. You people have a very beautiful mysticism but something is missing. The ogranizational content is missing. We must do something together. And the base communities must be places where the Sandinistas can go and help to organize the struggle."

At that time I was not ready to listen to that. And I said, "No, I'm not going to allow those who have no faith to use those who do. I know that we can go part of the way together, but then we split up. Your way and mine are different." He tried to convince me and finally said that I should consult with other priests.

So I did. I went to Masatepe to talk with my priest friends to explain Tomas's proposal to them but no one wanted to accept. Then I returned to Borge and said, "Nobody accepts." His response was, "There is a great bloodbath coming. And I warn you, it is necessary that Christians be involved in the struggle. You will have a great mission: when the temptation to be cruel comes to us, you are going to help to mitigate this cruelty."

Just recently, at a dinner in Los Rancho, Tomas reminded me of that conversation. "Remember, Uriel? I told you a bloodbath was coming. And I still say that Christians have a great role in this struggle."

Tomas Borge: I've had contact with Christianity from birth. I was even an altar boy as an adolescent. I was active in the Catholic church in Matagalpa. In fact my mother wanted me to be a priest. Uriel thought that I wanted to be a priest. But no, it was my mother. I decided not to.

Quite early on I began to think about things that went outside the framework of the church. I was astounded at the great contradiction involved in the existence of an infinitely just and kind God, with the terrifying conception of the hell described by the local bishop. I remember he used to stand there in the pulpit, and start talking about hell. And when he painted that incredible, unreal fire, I began to lose my fear of hell. I couldn't conceive of it. And that made me sceptical of religion. Then a different bishop came who I sympathized with; he was anti-Somoza.

Many years later I once again established contact with Christians through Ernesto Cardenal. He was the first priest I was in contact with. That was the first real connection between the Sandinista Front and revolutionary Christians. He spoke with us...it must have been in 1968 or 1969. I extended an invitation to him, through a letter which he kept but which later had to be burned for security reasons. It's too bad because it was a historical document. After I met with Ernesto we had another

Maria Hartman

meeting, which included Carlos Fonseca. Later came the relations with Uriel Molina and other Christian comrades. That's when we began to see Christianity from another perspective. We saw it as a different Gospel perspective; that is, Christ's option for the poor, the humble, the exploited. We talked to our militants about this.

I also always held the view that over the long term it is possible in Nicaragua for progressive Christians and revolutionaries to live together. The participation of the church seemed to me to be essential to avoid a situation where, after the fall of the tyranny, there might be a great bloodbath, a massacre. I said to Uriel that it was important for the church to participate in order to avoid a massacre of our people's enemies and to save the lives of many people. Hatred had accumulated for so many years and I was afraid that an uncontrollable violence would be unleashed against the *Somocistas*, the Guard. Uriel talked about our ways being different and that at one point we'd go our separate ways. But I held to the view that a lasting alliance, a strategic alliance, was possible.

Uriel: I didn't join quickly; I integrated myself into the struggle gradually. When that talk with Tomas Borge was over...and incidentally, they offered to take me to see Carlos Fonseca whom everyone thought was dead. I was afraid to go. I was dying to see him, but you had to change vehicles three times for security reasons. I would have to leave my own vehicle by a beer shop. I was somewhat afraid, and I never did see Carlos Fonseca.

But anyway, after that Christians fully joined the struggle of the Sandinista Front. It happened in various ways. For instance, Ernesto had already made his choice in Solentiname. He had published his *Psalms* and his *Gospel in Solentiname*. He had a deeper consciousness. Here the Sandinistas understood that I was not going to take the step of joining the guerrillas. And they accepted me like that.

I was always a religious leader. Revolutionary Christians

joined the Bible circles which were set up mostly for the youth, and then the community began a reactivation process through reading the Bible and having political discussion. That took place during 1974 and 1975. They would sing protest songs and talk about liberation. All that kept growing, 'til there was more and more political participation here in the community. By this time the old university community did not exist. The students had all gone underground, but the community lived on in the children, the old people, the men and the Christian youth.

During those months there would be deaths daily. I remember that in Rene Schick a woman called Bertha Calderon was killed and they buried her without a mass. When they had already buried her, a group of angry students asked, "Did you say a mass for her? If not, we're going to dig her up!"

So there was a big procession. People from our church said, "Father, the young people are coming. The church has to be opened so that a prayer can be said." I was scared to open the church because I thought the Guard would go in. But I went out to the garden and I saw the boys with the coffin on their backs...and the body was rotting, there was a stench of putrefaction...

"Father, open the door! Bertha cannot leave us until you say a prayer!" And it was so loud that I said, "All right, boys, we'll open the door." The body was brought in, and then I said, "I'm not just going to say a prayer, but a whole mass." And I put the vestments on and I began to cry with them. Everyone was crying. And that gave me a great courage. I felt that as a priest I had to take up that suffering. I believe that mass was one of the most beautiful I've given. It was a condemnation of the regime, violent and terrible. The boys went out happy. The carried the body in triumph.

Weeks and weeks went by, dead body after dead body. Dona Lolita Chavarria, a mother from the neighborhood, came to me crying. She'd found her son's body in a garbage dump, all in pieces. And the poor woman came to bury it, picking the bones and the skin.

Antonia: The most difficult period for the neighborhood began in 1977 with the first direct accusation against Father Uriel. He was accused of inducing young people to insurrection. They labelled him a "red priest".

Martha Cranshaw: I started university in 1972. My relation with the Front was not formalized at that point. I didn't even know that the comrades belonged to the Front. At this time the most advanced comrades in the Christian movement were directly linked to the Sandinista Front. Within about a year I had established links with the Front, through Monica.

When I went underground, all that my family knew was that I had been working in the "Open" *barrio*. "Open"

Tomas Borge

was a poor *barrio* on the outskirts of Managua, built after
the earthquake. It has now been renamed Ciudad Sandino.
They also knew I was close to Father Uriel Molina. I guess
it wasn't surprising that they'd look to those outside
influences as the cause for my "problem." They'd never
think that I had arrived at certain conclusions of my own
free will. They thought that an older person must have
influenced me. So my father focussed his anger on Father
Uriel Molina. That's when all eyes of repression were
focussed on Uriel anyway so when the argument blew up
between my father and Uriel it turned into a huge
discussion in the newspapers.

Uriel: I didn't realize that Martha Cranshaw had
disappeared. At that time many young people were
disappearing from their houses, and joining the Sandinistas in the underground. Eventually the word came that
Martha Cranshaw was a guerrilla in the mountains. Then
one day the National Guard found a guerrilla brigade with
Martha in it. They took her prisoner and brought her back
to Managua and to her father, the Director of Police.

Martha Cranshaw

Martha: My capture was reported in *La Prensa*. I had been condemned before being captured. I didn't go through the courts or give declarations. They brought me blindfolded into a room. Then when they took the blindfold off I saw all the newsmen. My family was also there. I hadn't seen them for a couple of years, so I didn't know how they were going to react. It wasn't the most appropriate time to talk things over. I think that despite everything I felt happy to see them. I cried, not because I was sorry for what I did but I felt such a mixture of feelings. It was a shock to see them so suddenly. That was the reason for the tears that the papers said were tears of repentance.

Uriel: She was very moved on seeing her family and her father. And Somoza, who knew about that, thought he would take advantage of the situation through a grand television show to the whole country. My mother was watching TV in the evening when suddenly Martha Cranshaw's father appeared on the screen. "Attention, we are going to give information denouncing the role played by a certain priest in our country." William Cranshaw appeared, and then his daughter Martha, with her head down. He embraced her while the television said, "This girl, who made the mistake of taking up arms, is today returning to her father and to her home, in repentance."

Then Cranshaw started to talk, saying that he was very happy to see his daughter but that he was very bitter about the fact that some priests are corrupting the Nicaraguan youth and sending them on the road to violence. "The worst one is Father Molina. It's time for us to start killing priests in this country." He said that right on television. When my mother heard that she was very upset. It was the first time anyone had talked about killing priests.

I was here at home when suddenly a group of about twenty newsmen appeared. I let them in and they said, "What do you think about Cranshaw's declaration? He is accusing you of indoctrinating the youth in Sandinista subversion." When it was clear I really didn't know what they were talking about they brought me a cassette so I could listen to what had been said.

Managua was so hot it was burning. From dawn on, people came to talk with me. At 9 a.m. Pedro Joaquin Chomorro came. He had written something defending me, but *La Prensa* was being censored. The bishop of Leon also sent a telegram of protest which wasn't published. And as if that wasn't enough, Martha's brother, William, who had been my student at the UCA, gave a news conference to all the journalists. He said it was true that his sister was deceived by Molina and other priests. "And we have to start killing them, beginning with those who wear a red sash." When he said "red sash" he distracted attention away from me without meaning to, and directed it to the bishop. Only bishops wear red sashes. So the journalists went to see the bishop. And when they asked Monsignor Obando about my being a communist, he said he didn't have any evidence of that.

Many priests who were very worried about me wanted to do something. We decided to celebrate a protest mass. You couldn't say anything in the newspapers or on the radio because everything was censored. So that night, one of the most beautiful ones of my life, they all came from Managua. The whole *barrio* was full of cars, over 30 priests came. And then I had the opportunity of celebrating a mass for the people, and in the sermon, which I still have, I defended my situation. I talked about why I had been called a communist. Fernando Cardenal also spoke that night. There were many testimonies, telegrams and letters from all the base communities.

Monsignor Obando decided not to be at the mass. The next day he called me to say he had received a letter from the Minister of Government Antonio Mora Rostran. It seems I was seriously implicated in Martha Cranshaw's declaration. The minister said they couldn't take responsibility for anything that might happen to me. When I saw that the minister wanted to blackmail the bishop by telling a lie and compromise the harmonious relations

David Chavarria Rocha

between the church and state I wrote the bishop a letter: "I
am ready to die rather than let you be stained by giving in
to blackmail by Somoza's government. He wants to blackmail you; instead I will go to the military courts to defend
myself." But he prohibited me from going to the courts. I
felt attacked from all sides. People would stare at me
everywhere, and I went through a period of real anguish.
But soon after the insurrection began. Martha disappeared
from her house again and did not reappear until the
Sandinista victory.

   The most beautiful case in the *barrio* was that of David,
a young person with a vocation to be a priest, a preacher, a
gentle man. Suddenly he disappeared and rumors started
about his being an informer. I could not believe that about
one of my boys...in fact David had started working very
closely as a collaborator with the Front, doing arms
transport across Managua.

David: I was working selling spare parts for cars. I would
finish at 4 or 5 p.m. and then go to the *barrio* to join the
activities, meetings and everything else that was happening
in the east end of Managua. At the beginning of 1973,
comrade Joaquin Cuadra asked me if I wanted to
collaborate with the Sandinista Front. I said yes, I'm
ready.

   To tell the truth, I was waiting for that. I had wanted to
contact someone but I didn't know who. I knew the work
we were doing was good, but it was not going to solve the
people's problems. The reformist struggle had a certain
sense for the people, but had been betrayed by the
conservative sector when Aguero, who had been elected on
a platform of opposition to Somoza in early 1967, made a
pact with the dictator. I stopped believing in civic opposition politics and parties then. That was just playing into
Somoza's hands. In this situation Somoza was getting
richer and richer, getting more ensconced in power. There
was no alternative but armed struggle.

   When I started working with the FSLN the first test they

gave me was to use my house as a safe house for two comrades. My family didn't know anything at the start. The comrades came and lived with us, but soon my mother found out they weren't just classmates of mine. There were lots of political papers in the house as well as the boards with nails that we used to puncture the tires of buses involved in the strike. She suspected our activities weren't exactly church business. She knew she'd been right when, three days after he left our house, comrade Aviles was assassinated in Nandaime. Like every other mother she was scared for me. She'd say, "Look, be careful, don't get involved in that"...the kinds of things mothers say who worry about their children.

I felt comrade Aviles's death very strongly, it pushed me to commit myself even more. We began to hold meetings, have study circles, form cells, and recruit more comrades from within and outside the youth movement for the Front's organizing work in the *barrio* and in the Maximo Jerez neighborhood. In 1974 there was an attack on Chema Castillo's house. After that, I found it hard to see anything but armed struggle as the alternative for the Nicaraguan people.

I participated in church activities more and more, because after the earthquake a new work system was instituted in the *barrio*, which was to go around all the *barrios* saying mass. Uriel and I would sometimes say three or four masses, two in the morning and two in the afternoon, and then do catechism with the children, go to the youth movement meetings and go to the base community meetings. I even went to the meetings for married couples sometimes. I had quite a hectic life, between my work, my classes, and my organizing work for the Front.

By then I had been integrated into the Front and was being assigned other jobs. The transport of comrades, keeping them in my house, organizing, recruitment, propaganda, painting slogans on walls, putting up banners...One time we put up a banner at the central

Alvaro Baltodano

police station.

I never felt far from the church. I had rediscovered within me a faith that was becoming more concrete, taking shape through practice.

Uriel: One day I was coming home around 10 at night and I saw the church door open. It was dark and I saw someone inside praying. When I came nearer, I realized it was David, after almost a year's absence. David embraced me; he was crying. He said, "I came to see you, because I have a sick heart. I think I killed someone. You have always taught us that life is sacred in the eyes of God. But last night I was driving a car taking arms to the east end. And when I passed the El Retiro hospital I saw a man waving to me. The curfew was on already so I couldn't stop, especially since my car was full of guns. Then I realized he was a Guard and from the way he walked he seemed drunk. I half-closed my eyes, stepped on the accelerator, and ran him over. I hit him hard. When I hit him your image came into my mind, and I couldn't help but come here, to cry and ask for your help." I asked him where the car was and he pointed just outside. I said, "For the Love of God stop praying, we have to do something with all the arms!" I went to ask some old ladies to help me out of the mess. I told them we were in danger and asked them to help transport the arms.

The next day we looked in the paper to see if there was news about a dead man. Nothing. But David would not calm down. So finally I went to look in all the hospitals. And in the Eastern Hospital I found a man who had been brought in the previous night with a broken skull. I went immediately to tell David he was still alive. I ended up looking after this sick man, who was a Guard and had no family. He hadn't died. I went every day to see that Guard. I said I was a priest visiting the sick. I lost touch with him because they transferred him to the military hospital where I couldn't go. I never knew if he lived or died. But David kept doing arms transport.

One day I turned the radio on to hear that David had been taken prisoner. Four security jeeps had pulled up to the shop where he worked and when the Guard asked if David lived there, the apprentices got nervous and said yes. Just then David came from the back of the shop. The guards jumped on him, beating him, and poor David fell down, half dead. They stuck him bleeding in a jeep, and took him to the security jail. We thought he wouldn't survive.

David: I never thought I'd come out of there alive. The Guard captured me and found everything we had at my place. They took me to the security offices and held me there for fifteen days. They tortured me and then transferred me to the central police station. They put me in with all the thieves and then into a cell called "the little one." That's where I had my first opportunity to write to Uriel, on a toilet paper wrapper. He read that letter to the community.

Uriel: When David was captured the community gathered immediately, the old women, everybody, to pray for David. We started a campaign of silent prayers, waiting for the right moment. As it happened David's mother was friends with the chief of security, Jiron. In Nicaragua there's a lot of that, people who know each other or are related, and she thought he would listen to her. She went everyday to the security offices and would stand there in the sun, crying. She didn't eat; she was fasting. And after thousands of tears a humble guard, who was one of the ones who took food into the prisoners, felt sorry for her. He went up to her and said, "Don't cry, today you will have news from your son." He told David his mother was outside. And then David was able to write me a letter, on toilet paper. When his mother saw the letter, she hid it and brought it to me.

It was so difficult to read that letter. He said, "I don't know if it's day or night. It's either terribly cold or

unbearably hot. A guy stepped on my genitals with his
military boots. He destroyed me. I am going to die. I don't
have the strength to live. But I want you to pray with the
community, and denounce these atrocities to the whole
world with the strength of your words. The world should
know what goes on here. I don't want anything else.''

When I read the letter we all cried. And I wondered:
Should I say these things publicly? They'll just kill him
faster. But the power of Christian testimony was the
stronger force. The next Sunday I denounced what was
going on. The church was full and we all prayed for David.

David: I had already left the community by the time I was
taken prisoner. Not because I didn't believe any more, but
because of the Front's activities. I would endanger those
comrades who had links with the parishes, in the youth
movement and in the base communities. But in the police
headquarters I felt the need to address myself to the
community and to Uriel, to tell them that I was still alive,
that I was in jail because of a cause, an act of faith. I had
to show him that I was putting up with it, and I was going
to hold on to the end. I hoped that this would be an
encouragement for other comrades, that it would help
raise their consciousness and also help to gain the support
of the people who were still not participating.

Uriel: I began writing him little letters using Biblical
language so that the Guard wouldn't suspect anything if
the letter fell into the hands of some lackey. And I sent him
the Eucharist and consecrated host* in a letter. And when
he received it he was happy.

He began such a beautiful dialogue from jail; I keep his
letters like treasures. He gave me strength and would say:
''We are going to win. We must have hope.'' He suffered a
great deal. Through understanding the incredible strength
of the guerrillas, of those who were tortured, I gained a
tremendous respect for them.

*The communion wafer.

I wanted to join the guerrillas too but I didn't have enough courage for that type of fight. Besides, it was clear that I had to remain at my post.

David: From the moment I wrote the letter and asked for it to be read in the community, I was ready to accept whatever came. I knew that when it was read there could be more repression. But I didn't care. What was important was for the community to use my capture as another means of denouncing the repressive and murderous regime of Somoza. In a way it was a privilege, when you are in a situation like that your testimony becomes very real and concrete. We have to be ready to give our lives for others.

Uriel: They had stripped him naked. One time he was facing the wall praying, and a guard came in and roughed him up. When he saw that David had a crucifix around his neck he tore off the cross and threw it on the ground. David said in a letter, "I never realized that I was naked, until they took my cross away." When you hear that, you think of Adam in the Book of Genesis where the Lord asks him, "Why did you hide?" and Adam says, "Because I felt I was naked." Before they took his cross, David didn't feel naked because he felt under Christ's shadow and protection. But when they took it away he felt completely abandoned. It's a very beautiful testimony of what faith is, in a fighter.

David: I got out with the amnesty of December, 1978. Or rather, a few days earlier, because my family paid money to some judge from Masaya so they would release me. Actually they released us because they knew the amnesty was imminent. The best thing for them was to take the money and let us go.

The first place I went was to the *barrio* to see Uriel and certain comrades who had shown solidarity with me in prison. And then, for security reasons, I had to go underground.

Uriel: When David got out of jail, I embraced him warmly. We were both crying. "Brother," he said to me, "I come to greet you and also to say goodbye. I'm saying it now so that you will be ready for the day when I go off to war." Then one morning David came by and left me a letter on the altar where I celebrate mass. It said, "Dear Uriel, my most important desire is for us to celebrate mass before I leave. I wanted to confess my sins. I wanted to say goodbye. I don't know if we'll see each other again, but I want to assure you that my faith will still be alive; in all fields of struggle, in the city or in the countryside. You have always been for me the union between God and people. And so today I write you this letter to deepen my communion with you. May the Lord bless you, and may the communion of the Holy Spirit be with you and with the whole community."

David: I was underground in Managua for about two months and then I went to the mountains. I took part in the freedom brigades, until July 19 when we entered Managua.

"Coco" Guerrero Lopez

We have to invent a new language to talk about God

Uriel: We have to learn a new language to talk about God. Up to now we have always talked about God in philosophical categories. When I studied theology the school of Thomas Aquinas was the intellectual school inside the church. When we dealt with the treatise about God it was said, in Latin: God is *ipsum, subsistens* which means that God is the being that subsists by itself, nothing else does. I didn't like that definition. In St. John's gospel he says "God is love." I thought this was too static a concept. Love cannot exist without a correlative, something that is loved. However, when I studied the Bible, the definitions contrasted with these. But in the Old Testament you constantly read the description of God not as a subsistent being but rather a man who is in love with a people whom he wants to save, like in a human love. There, the word God manifested as a liberating love for the poor and the oppressed, from the captivity in Egypt onward. That definition touched me profoundly. I felt that was closer to God. But there is another, superior, level still.

There is a future tense for the word. God does not say "I am," but "I will be." God is the future of life. I really like that concept. As Moses said to God, "I have the vision to lead my people to liberation, but how will they believe me? Who is it that sends me among them? Give me your name so that they will believe." And in accordance with their Hebrew mentality, God does not give his name. He says, "You just lead them. I will be he who will be. Now you do not know me, because I cannot give you a definition in terms of essence. I manifest myself in the event which will take place."

And so, when I talk about God now, I am talking about something that cannot be defined. I don't feel it as a presence or even see it visibly, but He was once made flesh in Jesus Christ. The Chilean theologian Gustavo Gutierrez said something which helped me in my search for God. He said, "Don't think that those who believe in God know what God is. The one who believes is the most unsure about what God is." We will have to learn to build a theology where the poor are an etymological mediation towards finding God. And for me that is fundamental.

Alvaro: Whether there was a God or not, wasn't the concern. The concern was the practical politics we were involved in and how our Christianity got expressed. For us to be Christian meant to work with those who were poorest and at that time it meant working with the Sandinista Front. That gave us the possibility of helping liberate the people and working towards a different world, the kind of world that the Bible talks about.

We read the Bible, studied liberation theology and discovered that if you really read the Bible with your eyes open you find that the history of the Hebrew people is a history of their fight for liberation. When you read about the life of Jesus Christ you realize that whether he was or

Christ is Coming, slogan of the counter-revolution

wasn't God, he was a man who was with the poor and who fought for the freedom of the poor.

For us the promised land was the freedom of the people. Of course, depending on the level of participation, people would look for more political explanations to guide their work and commitment. The question is not for anyone to come here and say whether the people in the Front believe in God or not. Each one believes in what he or she wants. But everyone has to fulfil a historic responsibility. That was our goal: to fulfil our historic responsibility.

Fernando: In 1970 or 1971 I had had a conversation with Commander Oscar Turcios. One thing he said was, "I don't care that you believe that there is another life after this one, or that you have other religious ideas. So it shouldn't matter to you that I believe that this life is all there is. What should matter to both of us is that we can work together to build a new nation." I was in complete agreement.

Roberto: I think that sometimes it's posed to suggest that to be a believer you have to believe in God and in a bunch of dogmas postulated by the Catholic church. If being a believer is believing in the sort of God who talks to you, then I'm not one. But I do feel that people have to believe in something, and I think that we were successful in contextualizing that belief.

I don't know exactly when I stopped believing in the God we had been told about since we were born. I never really had a crisis of faith. It was a process in which I came to see logically what it was that I believed at the time. I never felt I had to choose rationally. I think my faith was transformed into something else, into political conscious-ness, the revolutionary experience, Sandinismo.

Alvaro: It's not important whether or not you are a Christian. I am not a believer now, not because the revolution has turned me into a non-believer but because I have other concerns. That Nicaraguans have more freedom, more independence, more sovereignty. That every day there be less injustice. That economic development be achieved. That all countries in the world be liberated. Those are my concerns.

If that's being a Christian, then fine. No problem. Our transformation went from religious training, to social concerns, through personal struggle, and finally a political transformation which led us to joining the Front. The Front allowed us to develop as Christians and revolutionaries.

Joaquin: The experience of faith lasts even when you begin to question the validity of paternalistic work. I did start to have a crisis and to think that I might not need a faith, but then we went to the community. In the early period of the community we still expressed the experience of faith; we had our own masses. That was the basis on which I built my revolutionary mysticism. For instance, I had not known heroic examples of comrades whose example could serve as the basis to nourish my mysticism. I didn't know

Christian base communities in Managua demand
more official church support for the Revolution

that. The mysticism I gained was based on my faith experience, which, through revolutionary militancy, was substituted by a revolutionary mysticism.

Salvador: I never had a motivation like that, though there were some religious and faith elements. My development came more gradually as my political consciousness came to predominate over my religious motivation. At no given point did I have to choose to abandon my faith.

David: I consider myself a Christian but not subject to all the traditions and myths of many believers. That kind of faith makes an easy target for the manipulations of certain reactionary sectors that want to use religious questions to create problems for the revolutionary process. I consider myself a Christian, but I am clear that if at any moment I have to choose between religion and revolution, I'd choose revolution.

Monica: I didn't come to believe in armed struggle in one day; it wasn't like that with my faith, either. I didn't say one day: today I don't believe. No. When I was in the underground I still read the Bible and prayed. I still feel very close to those who believe. I know their language and I have a great respect for them because of my training, and for many other reasons. I wouldn't say I am an atheist or antigod. Our people are a religious people. I can go to mass, still make the sign of the cross or kneel with the people. I respect those who believe. As a Sandinista leader I don't see anything there against our principles. Perhaps I don't believe in God because I've studied a little bit of science and because I have no need to believe in God.

When people from outside ask me whether I have been discriminated against because of my faith, I say no. And when they ask what base community I belong to, I say that I don't belong to any, that I am a professional of the Sandinista Front. I'm not going to lie and say that I pray in a community when it's not true.

Captain Jose Antonio Sanjines: A revolutionary is someone who has faith in life, in the fact that there is a meaning in life, which is the struggle for revolution. He is a man who even feels a faith in victory so that he sacrifices his own life understanding the transcendence of that. He understands that life itself is contained within the life of a people, the life of humanity.

I believe that in practice there are a lot of similarities between the revolutionary and the true believer: mysticism, discipline, sacrifice.

Coco: Before I lived in this *barrio*, I thought of God as a punishing God. When you're little they tell you: God is going to punish you. But then I discovered the real God of the Bible, for example in the Book of Exodus, when He takes his people out of oppression. It's still the same God, but now He doesn't prevent me from seeing reality, seeing oppression. On the contrary: the faith that I have is telling me that I should get involved, even if it's to do the minimum. How can I say it? I believe in the liberating God. Not the God who flatters and manipulates, but the God who is going to transform not just me, but a whole society. We are going to share Him and live Him. He belongs to all of us. That's my God.

A church transforming itself

Fernando: Until now all revolutions have opposed the church, because the church has been against all revolutions. Here we have for the first time an instance where the church is not only not against the revolution, but is completely in favor of it and supports it. We see that this profound unity is an example, and is motivating people in El Salvador, Guatemala and other countries. In this way we are destroying the idea that a Christian can't be a revolutionary.

I've always had a desire to dedicate my life to service. I

haven't changed that attitude. *I am completely clear that the greatest service I can do for this people is to participate in the revolution as one more soldier who is ready to carry out any mission.* For me, the priesthood is, above all, a service. I don't have a purely formal or cultural conception of the priesthood. It is giving, giving oneself to the people to serve in the building of a new community, a new homeland, a new man with new values.

Some people ask how a priest can be directly involved in a revolution. They should ask how a priest could have worked as I did before. The Jesuits have always held that teaching is one of the most important tasks. Comrades of mine used to teach English their whole lives; teachers of mine taught algebra for 50 years. I used to teach philosophy at the university: the ideas of Plato, Aristotle, Descartes, etc. Really, I don't think that was so priestly. But nobody ever objected to that. When we joined the revolution, then they started to ask if that was priestly or not. To teach our people how to read, to make over a half a million Nicaraguans literate, I don't know why that's not priest-like enough for some! But to teach 40 upper-class boys English was not seen as a problem. This is another sign of the depth of class struggle; in many cases morality fits the class of the preacher. According to these gentlemen it's bad that I've joined the revolution because it goes against their class interests.

Here in Nicaragua we have broken with all that. It is the people who have shown us by example that you can be both Christian and revolutionary.

David: I no longer worry about the doctrines of the church, but only about the church defending class privileges and attitudes. Even now, after the victory, the bishop has not been able to go to the poor sectors. Our leaders have gone there, and have solved problems and have heard the concerns of our people. Obando has not been able to do that. He has divorced himself from the popular masses, from the church, from the poor, from the

Christians who live and suffer everyday, from the crisis that imperialism and its lackeys are causing in Nicaragua. For me, he has lost credibility.

We have seen from him an attitude of trying to confuse the people, trying to make trouble, trying to manipulate the power to make decisions and the authority that the archbishop has as the leader of the church. There cannot be a church of the rich. Christ was the first to accuse the rich, telling them that it was easier for a camel to go through the eye of a needle than for a rich man to enter the kingdom of Heaven.

Roberto: The ideological hegemony that Monsignor Obando has as a person and as an institution has for the first time met a challenge in Sandinismo. The ideological hegemony of Sandinismo does not necessarily imply a decline in the religiosity of the people. But it gives a different content to it. In any case, this shouldn't be seen as a competition, but unfortunately that's how Monsignor Obando sees it.

Secondly, I think that a political and ideological class problem is being formulated by a certain sector in the hierarchy. There is a social section of the petit bourgeoisie that hesitates, that is reformist, that has not taken a stand in respect to the revolution. They are afraid of the historic project of the people. They are afraid of Sandinismo, and have reformist illusions.

Some parts of the bourgeoisie were revolutionary in that they helped to overthrow the dictatorship, but their structural ideological position was reactionary. Now, the correlation of forces has made them change, because there is no hope now of making a reactionary ideology stick, and so they have to turn to reformism. This is the point in which the bourgeois opposition and the hierarchy of the church come together: they completely agree about their reformist illusions, and are united in this.

Joaquin: It might be worthwhile for you to take the time to count how many members of the Sandinista Assembly took their first political steps in the Christian youth movement. This would give you a sense of the importance of the Christian movement for our revolution.

The fact that there was a strong Christian revolutionary movement at the base level is also very important. This movement is broad-based, has a defined revolutionary position and plays a very important support role inside the revolution. In every working class neighborhood of Managua there are Christian communities. On the other hand, there is the position against the revolution that is being taken more openly every day by the high clergy, who undoubtedly have some influence with our people, especially in the least politicized Christian sectors.

I believe that the Sandinista Front has to have an intelligent policy about this. It would be counterproductive for us to fall into their traps or to encourage a confrontation with the bishops which would only lead to a polarization within the church, and perhaps eventual division into two churches. Then the government would be forced to say: well, the church that we recognize is this one, and let the others go. This would have a great impact on international relations. We don't need this now, especially during these moments of danger. We have to unite our forces, to unify different sectors in the defense of our country. But I think that the division may have to happen some day. We have to make sure that it happens at the most convenient time, and with the least repercussions.

We can't manage these things indefinitely. Historically, a moment will come for a parting of ways. We will have to make a choice, even at the level of relations with the Vatican. If there was a provocation in that sense, as I said before, it would have a lot of repercussions internationally and at this point be counterproductive.

What is real is the support for the revolution given by the more conscious Christian sectors of our people. They support the revolution even because of their class intuition. They are religious, they respect Monsignor

Obando; perhaps they still believe in Our Lady of Cuapa, who appears to people from time to time. But the main point is the popular support given by those people for the revolution.

Alvaro: The Front has always said: we respect and encourage the traditions of our people. We respect the beliefs of our people, and allow them to develop. In the Front we have Christians who are militants, not only priests but also practicing Christians. For instance, my father. He is a militant in the Front and is a Christian. He believes that Christianity has to be integrated into the revolution. And my father is in the Christian movement.

David: I don't see any difference or any contradiction between Marxism and Christianity. We saw in Christian life a model for society, where everyone would have what was just, what was necessary, living without humiliation and according to their needs. If socialism is a just distribution of the goods and resources of the country for the benefit of the majority of the people, then I don't see any contradiction between Christianity and socialism. I *do* see a contradiction between Christianity and capitalism which oppresses and exploits and uses marginalization and repression.

Tomas: It has been shown that revolutionary Christians and revolutionaries who are not Christians can have a common path. What opened up the possibility of that strategic alliance was the honesty of the priests I have mentioned, their identification with the poor, their consistency with the Christian Gospel. Some say that these priests are Marxists disguised as Christians. That's false. They are true Christians. They really do believe in the life to come, they do believe in Christ, they do believe in their religion. That's the truth. And despite that, or perhaps because of it, they are identifying themselves with the poor.

And then, there is a whole series of Christian virtues which are identical with revolutionary virtues. For example, modesty. Real humility, not the false humility sometimes preached in the churches. Not the humility that wants to be elevated to sainthood, but the true humility preached and practiced by Jesus Christ, and that we have seen in men who are so true to those principles, for instance Fernando.

Fernando Cardenal, in my judgment, is the archetype of what a Christian should be. There you will find true modesty, without any gilding, without any gold rings for other people to kiss. Fernando was the real architect of the national literacy crusade, and he never bragged about it. Never! He even tried to hide his work so it wouldn't be noticed. He never went around claiming to be a prophet. That's a true Christian. And a true revolutionary. And Fernando is not a Marxist disguised as a Christian. He is a Christian.

Maria: What has happened in the church would have been impossible 20 or 30 years ago. What has happened to the church in Latin America is extraordinary. I think about that when I go to the U.S. and see how the church is there. I think: you are so backward! And they never believe me. Because they think about the "third world," and assume we are underdeveloped. But as far as the church is concerned, my god, we are very developed! And then I have a great hope. We only started organizing the *barrio* in 1972. It was so difficult. And the people were scared, you know? The struggle of all these years. And afterwards, just like that, we had the war: and it was all over. Everything went so quickly towards the end, that it seemed almost incredible. I believe that in the church it will be the same thing. . .

Chronology

1522-24   Conquest of Nicaragua by the Spanish, bringing with them the first Catholic priests.

1550   (Feb. 26) For his defence of the Indians, Bishop Fray Antonio Valdivieso is stabbed to death by an agent of an aristocratic family. He is the first martyr of the Nicaraguan church. After the FSLN victory in 1979 the Antonio Valdivieso Ecumenical Centre was opened.

1823   (Dec. 2) U.S. government announces Monroe Doctrine declaring Latin America to be in its "sphere of influence."

1838   Nicaragua becomes an independent state.

1855   First American military intervention, a non-governmental one led by pro-confederate William Walker.

1856   Walker declares himself president of Nicaragua and is immediately recognized by the U.S. government. He is ousted in 1857 by joint efforts of Central American states, Britain, U.S. railroad magnate Cornelius Vanderbilt, and Nicaraguan Conservatives.

1857-93   Nicaragua governed by Conservative Party.

1909   U.S. Marines intervene to assure success of Conservative rebellion against Liberal president Jose Santos Zelaya. Civil war ensues.

1912   2,700 U.S. Marines end civil war, massacring 600 supporters of General Benjamin Zeledon, "El Indio."

1925   Creation of the National Guard.

1926   Renewed civil war leads to new U.S. intervention (4,000 troops).

1927   U.S. presidential envoy imposes pact on warring parties, including reorganization of National Guard under U.S. control. Pact opposed by Liberal General Augusto Cesar Sandino, who forms Army in Defence of National Sovereignty (2 Sept.).

1927-32   War between Sandino's troops and U.S.

1933   (1 Jan.) Unable to defeat Sandino, U.S. troops withdraw, having first appointed Anastasio Somoza Garcia head of National Guard.

1934   (21 Feb.) Sandino assassinated by National Guard.

1936   Somoza elected president.

1956   (21 Sept.) Assassination of Somoza Garcia by poet Rigoberto Lopez Perez. Somoza is succeeded by his son Luis. Younger son Anastasio Somoza Debayle is already head of National Guard.

1959   Cuban Revolution.

1960   Formation of first Christian base communities in Latin America (especially in Brazil).

1961   U.S. forms Alliance for Progress. Attempted CIA-Cuban exile invasion of Cuba defeated at Playa Giron (Bay of Pigs). During the invasion bombing raids on Cuba are launched from Nicaragua; landing craft debark from Nicaragua's east coast.

(July) Formation of *Frente Sandinista para la Liberacion Nacional* (FSLN).

1962-65   Second Vatican Council (Vatican II) called by Pope John XXIII undertakes a series of church reforms (including mass in the vernacular) and moves the church towards an understanding that it is part of history, not outside or above it.

1963   Luis Somoza hands over power to Rene Schick, a friend of the family. Anastasio Somoza remains head of National Guard.

1966   Father Ernesto Cardenal and William Agudelo begin Solentiname community.

1965-66   Camilo Torres, the first Latin American priest to take up arms against dictatorship, joins guerrillas in Colombia and is killed.

1967   Anastasio Somoza Debayle elected president of Nicaragua following massacre of demonstrators by National Guard. In August, the first sustained military action of the FSLN takes place in Pancasan, near Matagalpa. Following its retreat, the FSLN begins underground work in urban *barrios*. In October, Cuban revolutionary Che Guevara is killed in Bolivia. His tiny guerrilla group is wiped out.

1968   Latin American bishops meet at Medellin, Colombia, to apply the concepts of Vatican II to Latin America. The Medellin documents contain an analysis of the suffering of Latin Americans under repressive political and economic conditions. They predict "uprisings of despair unless this suffering is alleviated."

In Nicaragua, Capuchin priests in the eastern province of Zelaya create the first course for lay ministers and local community leaders, who are called "Delegates of the Word."

1968-70 Christian base communities begin to develop in the poorer neighborhoods of Managua and other cities.

1969   Jesuits found CEPA (Evangelical Committee for Agrarian Progress) to work in rural communities.

1970-72 Occupations of churches throughout the country by people demanding an end to the repression and freedom for political prisoners.

1971   A dozen university students go to live with Father Uriel Molina at his parish in El Riguero, a working class neighborhood of Managua.

1972-79 Growing contact and discussion between Christian base communities and the Christian Youth Movement on the one hand, and the FSLN on the other, leading to collaboration in common struggle to liberate the country.

1973   Democratically elected socialist government of Salvador Allende overthrown by Chilean military.

1974   FSLN returns to major military action with an attack on the house of Chema Castillo, Somoza's minister of agriculture, holding hostages for 60 hours and winning several major demands.

Somoza declares state of siege that lasts for 33 months. National Guard begins widespread peasant massacres in an attempt to crush Sandinista popular support.

1975   FSLN splits into three tendencies: Prolonged People's War, Proletarians, and Insurrectionals (or *Terceristas*).

1976   Capuchin fathers denounce mass murders and torture of peasants in northern part of the country.

1977-79   Nicaragua's Conference of Bishops, led by Archbishop Obando y Bravo, produces a series of pastoral letters denouncing the dictatorship and condoning the people's right to struggle. A letter of Aug. 3, 1978 calls for Somoza's resignation. A letter of July 2, 1979 (17 days before victory) supports the people's right to insurrection ("the just war"). A letter of November, 1979 basically supports the new government, though with reservations. From then to the present, Obando y Bravo and most bishops have grown increasingly critical of the revolution.

1977   Father Fernando Cardenal testifies before a U.S. Congressional subcommittee on peasant massacres in Zelaya. In October, the Insurrectional group of the FSLN attacks three National Guard posts, including San Carlos, where the attack is conducted by members of Ernesto Cardenal's Solentiname community.

Shortly after, twelve leading Nicaraguans (*Los Doce*), including priests Fernando Cardenal and Miguel D'Escoto, issue a statement saying there can be no solution to the country's problems without the participation of the FSLN in government and an end to the dictatorship.

On Dec. 25, Spanish-born priest Gaspar Garcia Laviana writes a letter to Nicaraguans explaining how his Christian commitment has led him to join the FSLN. Almost a year later he is killed in battle.

1978   (Jan.) Assassination of Pedro Joaquin Chamorro, publisher of *La Prensa*. Consequent riots and first business strike against Somoza.

(Feb.) Partial insurrection in Indian *barrio* of Monimbo.

(July) Somoza is unable to prevent the return of *Los Doce* to Nicaragua, where they are greeted by huge demonstrations.

(Aug.) FSLN commando takes over the National Palace, winning freedom for political prisoners and many other demands, including a rise in the minimum wage.

(Sept.) Insurrection in seven cities put down by National Guard bombing of residential areas and markets, followed by vicious repression.

1979   (Jan.) After a year of strong debate and disagreement, Latin American bishops meet at Puebla, Mexico. They adopt a "preferential option for the poor" which, though open to different interpretations, strengthens the position of base communities and those Catholics working for social change.

(Mar.) Formal unification of the FSLN. First major military action involving combatants of all three tendencies.

(29 May) Opening of FSLN's final offensive with the entry of the Benjamin Zeledon Front in the south of the country.

(19 July) Surrender of the National Guard. FSLN columns enter Managua to join with urban insurrection. Victory of Nicaraguan revolution. Four priests, Miguel D'Escoto, Ernesto Cardenal, Fernando Cardenal, and Edgar Parrales, are given important posts in the new government despite Vatican disapproval. A fifth priest, Alvaro Arguello, represents Nicaraguan clergy in the Council of State. In 1980, after a series of demands from the Vatican and the bishops that they resign their posts, the four announce their intention to remain in the government.

1980   (Mar. 24) Assassination of El Salvador's Archbishop Oscar Arnulfo Romero while saying mass. A week earlier he had called on Salvadoran troops to disobey their officers and stop the murder of thousands in that country.

(Oct.) FSLN issues statement on religion, pledging total freedom of belief, expression and practice and recognizing the role of Christians in the struggle for liberation and their right to membership in the FSLN. In response the Nicaraguan Episcopal Conference produces a pastoral letter denouncing the assault of materialism on the church in Nicaragua.

Salvadoran National Guard murders four American missionaries, nuns Ita Ford, Maura Clarke and Dorothy Kazel and lay worker Jean Donovan.

1980-83   Growing tensions between church hierarchy and popular movement in Nicaragua. Harassment of priests and nuns who are part of the people's struggles by Obando y Bravo and other bishops. Priests are removed from their parishes, some are sent out of the country. Monsignor Jose Arias Caldera of Santa Rosa is given notice to leave his church; the parishioners protest and they are excommunicated by Obando y Bravo.

1983   (Mar.) Pope John Paul II visits Nicaragua. Eight hundred thousand people attend open-air mass, including mothers of 17 young people who had been buried the day before after dying fighting against ex-National Guard. The Pope's answer to the mothers' request for a prayer for peace is "Silence." In a speech in Managua, the Pope attacks the revolution and offers support to Obando y Bravo.

The FSLN reiterates its commitment to religious freedom and expresses confidence that what the Pope saw in Nicaragua will help him evaluate the Central American situation.

About the Author

Poet, translator, editor, political analyst and photographer, Margaret Randall was born in New York City in 1938 and grew up in New Mexico. In 1961 she moved to Mexico City where she founded and co-edited the literary magazine *El Corno Emplumado/The Plumed Horn*. From 1969 to 1981 she lived and worked in Cuba and in 1981 she moved to Nicaragua. In early 1984 she returned to live in the United States. Margaret Randall's books include *Women in Cuba, Cuban Women Now, With Our Hands, Spirit of the People, Carlota: Prose and Poetry from Cuba,* and *Breaking the Silences.* Since the late 1970s she has worked extensively in a literary form that is part oral history, part interview, part essay; the result has been three books about Nicaragua, *Doris Tijerino: Inside the Nicaraguan Revolution* (1978), *Sandino's Daughters* (1981) and *Christians in the Nicaraguan Revolution* (1983).